5-Minute Mindfulness
for Raising Toddlers

5-MINUTE MINDFULNESS

FOR

raising toddlers

SIMPLE PRACTICES TO MANAGE STRESS AND FIND CALM

STACY SPENSLEY

ROCKRIDGE PRESS

Interior and Cover Designer: Alan Carr
Art Producer: Samantha Ulban
Editor: Olivia Bartz
Production Manager: Riley Hoffman

All Images Used Under License Shutterstock and iStock. Author Photo Courtesy of Sophia Mavrides

Paperback ISBN: 978-1-63878-338-1
eBook ISBN: 978-1-63878-538-5
R0

FOR MY KIDS,
who are my greatest teachers.

AND FOR MY GROUP CHATS,
who are my biggest cheerleaders.

contents

introduction

Welcome! I'm so grateful that you picked up this book. As a mom of three kids and as a parenting coach with more than a decade of client experience, I'm no stranger to the joys and challenges of parenting. My oldest was a high-needs baby at a time when my husband had to work extremely long hours. Though toddlerhood is one of my favorite ages, it was a huge transition for everyone. Currently, I'm wrapping up my third round of the toddler years, and I've learned (and taught a lot of other caregivers) strategies and techniques to navigate them.

If you're struggling with that transition, you're not alone. Toddlers' brains are rapidly developing, but they don't yet have logic or reasoning skills. They do, however, have intense feelings, which can cause overwhelm and stress. Whether you're home with your child or your child is in childcare while you work, each situation presents plenty of challenges. It can be draining to constantly juggle life demands and then hold space for your toddler, too.

Raising kids might be the biggest personal development project you can undertake, sometimes in unexpected ways. When you try to manage your child's big feelings, you first have to manage your own—but you may not have learned how. This can cause you to parent based on your past or in response to your fears about the future. Being constantly busy and stressed can also drain you of patience and calm. That's where mindfulness comes in. Mindfulness is simply a state of being aware of the present moment and acknowledging your thoughts and feelings without judgment. When you can meet yourself where you are, you're better able to be and parent the way you want.

When I was struggling to navigate my oldest child's transition into toddlerhood, I read a lot of books and articles. Most information on the toddler years focuses on children's behavior, but the recommended responses assume the parent or caregiver can stay calm. Toddlers push buttons like it's their job, and staying calm after your little one throws a block at your head like a future major league pitcher is not easy. I felt like most of what I read was about staying calm but didn't actually offer strategies on how to do that. The defiance and risk-taking of toddlerhood is entirely different than dealing with a baby. That's where mindfulness is a powerful strategy for helping you stay calm and present instead of reactive. It's not about pushing your own feelings down; rather, it's about acknowledging them when they arise and letting them go.

Starting a mindfulness practice can sound overwhelming, especially for parents who are often busy, burned out, and straight up exhausted. That's why this book has a wide variety of options for mindfulness practices that take five minutes or fewer. Just a few minutes of mindfulness can offer support, and many of the practices can be done with or next to your child.

While mindfulness is an incredible tool to help manage anxiety and stress, it is not meant to replace therapy, medical care, or medication. If you have breathing issues, use caution or consult your doctor before starting breathwork practices. If you feel dizzy, lightheaded, or anxious during an activity, stop that activity immediately. Caregivers with disabilities or a history of trauma may want to consult a care provider for additional guidance. If you are struggling with postpartum mood or anxiety disorder symptoms, anxiety, or depression, you also need the right support. Please see the Resources section at the end of this book for resources for professional help.

It can feel overwhelming to start a new practice. It can be uncomfortable to try new things and feel like you're not good at them yet. But you cannot do this wrong. If all you can do in a day is take one breath, pause for one moment, or take one mindful bite of food, that's the first step. Like compounding interest, the benefits increase exponentially over time.

how to use this book

Reading this book is the first step toward mindfulness, but you have to implement what you learn. That may mean consistently setting aside time each day or finding the rhythm that works with your life. My hope is that practicing mindfulness becomes a habit for you that gets easier over time.

The first part of this book summarizes the history and benefits of mindfulness, followed by how the practice supports parents of toddlers. The second part consists of eight themed chapters featuring a variety of five-minute mindfulness exercises. Topics include calming your mind, checking in with your body, connecting with your child, dealing with complicated emotions, and making the most of daily routines.

Each practice can be done in five minutes or fewer, though you may want to spend more time if you have it. Many of the practices are conveniently structured to do with, or at least near, your toddler. If you're very new to mindfulness, it may help to begin by repeating one exercise until you feel more confident. If you need novelty, you may prefer to try something new each day.

Any new practice is a challenge at first, and it can feel uncomfortable and messy to sit with your thoughts if you're not used to it. With a toddler, it may not be realistic to commit to a daily mindfulness practice right away, but once a week may work right now. If you miss a day, just notice those feelings and recommit to practicing the next day. The goal isn't to work through the book and do every practice; it's to imbue your life with more mindful moments and provide a range of ideas to help you get started.

PART I

AN INTRODUCTION TO MINDFULNESS

You may already have some sense of what mindfulness is, but in this section, we will delve into its origins and evolution. You don't need to understand all of the science behind mindfulness to reap its benefits. Chapter 1 will cover its development and a variety of practices in order to provide the context and background for the practices in part 2.

Developing a mindfulness practice doesn't have to be time consuming, and there are both immediate and long-term effects.

Once you know the origins of the practice, chapter 2 covers the joys (and stresses) of toddlerhood, and how mindfulness can support parenting at this stage. We'll look at how a mindfulness practice can help you and your child. And most importantly, we'll look at how to make this happen when you're trying to keep an adorable, rapidly developing ball of energy alive and fed.

Are you ready?

Mindfulness 101

"Mindfulness" can seem like a vague term, so let's establish what it is and what it isn't. Where did it come from, and how did it get here? Don't worry, there's no quiz at the end, but it's important to understand and honor the origins of the practice to fully receive its benefits.

There are various forms of mindfulness to consider; if one modality doesn't work for you, there are options. The benefits of mindfulness vary, from physiological changes visible in 60 seconds to long-term improvements in mental and physical health.

There are also challenges to starting a mindfulness practice. We'll look at what they are and how to address them. You'll get tips to get started, signs that your practice is working, and what to focus on if you can only do the bare minimum.

It can be tempting to want all the answers: for a book to tell you exactly what to do, for how long, and how many times a week in order to achieve a certain result. It would be easier if everything were like that, including parenting! Mindfulness is a journey that is uniquely yours, and one that will develop and change as you grow your practice. This book will provide you with the tools to get you started, but please keep in mind that there's no right or wrong path or pace, and progression usually isn't linear. Setbacks and challenges are part of the experience. You're already taking the first step by reading this book.

What Is Mindfulness?

Mindfulness, at its core, is being present in the moment, physically, mentally, and emotionally. Many of us were raised to ignore or bottle up feelings to protect the feelings of others or to avoid appearing "weak." Mindfulness is a tool to honor and reconnect to your physical sensations, thoughts, and feelings as they are, with awareness and curiosity, not judgment.

Everyone has their own base level of observation called "dispositional mindfulness." According to a 2015 study published in *Social Cognitive and Affective Neuroscience*, participants who had stronger dispositional mindfulness traits showed increased activity in multiple areas of the brain's cortex (which manages stress reactions) and less activity in the amygdala (which detects stress). What does that indicate? The better you are at being present and noticing your thoughts and feelings, the better you are at self-regulation. Other research has also shown that mindfulness improves memory and the ability to process information to make decisions.

The good news is that mindfulness is like a muscle that can grow stronger through practice. Adverse childhood experiences and other trauma, anxiety, depression, and some neurotypes such as attention-deficit hyperactivity disorder (ADHD) can affect activity in the amygdala, so it's possible that they affect dispositional mindfulness base levels as well. If you fall in one of those categories and find that mindfulness is a big challenge, remember that it gets easier as you grow your practice.

WHAT MINDFULNESS ISN'T

It's important to clarify that mindfulness is NOT "emptying your mind" or "not thinking." It isn't a specific practice, doesn't need to be done in a particular place, and doesn't require a long stretch of time. You don't have to sit still, be in a class, or acquire any equipment. The only thing you need is yourself.

Mindfulness is a practice and will never be perfect. In fact, a healthy mindfulness practice involves growth and change over time. It's not a magic button. Although its effects can be quite substantial, it can't entirely replace other modalities of treatment, but it can work alongside them.

The Origins and Evolution of Mindfulness

Though mindfulness does not require any type of spiritual practice, its roots are found in Asian philosophy and religion. The Vedic and yoga teachings of Hinduism are difficult to trace to a single point, but they have included mindfulness for thousands of years. British writers coined the term "Hinduism" in the 1800s in what is modern-day Pakistan and India. Buddhism began around 400 BCE in what is now Nepal. Some consider the word *mindfulness* to be a simplified translation of *Sati*, the first step to Buddhist enlightenment.

These ideas have been practiced for millennia by Hindus and Buddhists, but they became better known in the United States in the 1970s, based on the work of Thích Nhất Hạnh and Jon Kabat-Zinn. Thích Nhất Hạnh was a Buddhist monk living in France who wrote a considerable amount about mindfulness. One of his students, Jon Kabat-Zinn, opened the Center for Mindfulness at the University of Massachusetts Medical School and the Oasis Institute for Mindfulness-Based Professional Education and Training.

In 1979, Kabat-Zinn launched the Mindfulness-Based Stress Reduction (MBSR) program, an 8-week meditation and yoga course designed for hospital patients with a variety of health issues to reduce stress. Compared to many medical interventions, a mindfulness practice was non-invasive, low-risk, and inexpensive. The practice was meant to be educational, not directly therapeutic, yet patients with a wide range of ailments saw improvement in their mental and physical health.

Since then, hundreds of studies have been conducted using MBSR with healthy people, cancer patients, nurses, people with depression and anxiety, and other health conditions. Many of the studies were relatively small, but meta-analyses have found a consistent correlation between mindfulness interventions and a reduction in stress levels across the research population.

The low cost and accessibility of mindfulness programs make them a popular choice for attempting to individually address the increases in stress and anxiety caused by larger systemic issues.

Types of Mindfulness

There's no single or "right" way to practice mindfulness. The basic premise is simply to be present and aware, and there are many ways to do that. If you've tried one approach that didn't work, try another. It's called a *practice* for a reason.

Everyone's brain works a little differently, or you may simply have different needs at different times in your life. Many factors can influence which type of meditation you are drawn to. For example, some of the more popular or common types of meditation may not work as well for people with ADHD or other types of neurodiversity.

Meditation is only one way to practice mindfulness. There are many other ways to incorporate mindful practices into your day. Choose one that works for you, or one that you haven't tried before. There can be overlap. (There are types of meditation that include visualization or movement, for example.) Try out these tools and notice how they make you feel.

MEDITATION

Meditation is probably the most well-known type of mindfulness practice. At its core, meditation is a set of techniques to increase concentration and awareness. While there are many types of meditation, it most often involves a practice of sitting still, focusing on the breath, and noticing thoughts as they come up. This can be done on your own or in a group. You can meditate silently or with a guided meditation track of music, words, or both.

Mindful meditation is a specific practice, but there are also loving-kindness meditations, body scan meditations, transcendental or mantra meditations, or more structured spiritual practices like Zen meditation or Kundalini yoga.

A basic meditation practice can reduce your heart rate, blood pressure, and stress levels. Some can reduce pain levels, increase focus and concentration, improve memory, and lessen emotional reactivity.

VISUALIZATION

Visualization can be done on its own or as part of a guided meditation. It can be described as playing a video in your head, either of a peaceful place or of an event as you want it to happen in the future.

A common example of visualization is when athletes picture themselves making the shot or winning their race. Another is seeing yourself give a successful presentation. Doing something new or unknown can increase stress, but creating an image of an achievement can help build neural patterns in your brain as if you have already done it.

Picturing the activity going well can help regulate your nervous system and decrease anxiety. Visualization can also help improve focus and productivity since you've gone through the steps of what you want to happen in your mind already.

GENTLE MOVEMENT

Physical stillness is not a requirement for mindfulness. Stress shows up in both the mind and the body. The key to mindful movement is keeping your focus on your body and your experience in the present. Yoga is a great example of a gentle, mindful movement practice. Other guided movements include the flowing motions of tai chi or repeated gestures of qi gong.

Some activities may not automatically be mindful but can be done mindfully. Walking, hiking, paddleboarding, kayaking, canoeing, and swimming are great examples. You can also be mindful while washing the dishes, painting, knitting, or gardening. Mindfulness can be applied to a variety of hobbies or activities you already do.

The benefits may include improved range of motion, reduced stress and anxiety, a stronger immune system, and improved focus.

BREATHWORK

You might think that breathing is an automatic biological process, and you're partially right. The trick is that your breath also changes based on stimuli and stress, and it can trigger other physiological responses. If you adapt to a consistent high level of stress, your natural breathing patterns can change without you noticing, causing physical symptoms and anxiety.

When you perceive a threat (your ancestors might have faced a wild animal, whereas you might face a work deadline, paying bills on a limited income, or a toddler having big feelings), your breathing gets faster to get more oxygen into your bloodstream as quickly as possible in case you need to run. This can become a cycle where you experience stress, start to breathe quickly, and produce cortisol and adrenaline. You continue the shallow breathing, so your body thinks you're still in danger. The cortisol and adrenaline trigger shallow breathing. Repeat. This is especially true when you face multiple stressors, which most people do trying to juggle kids and life.

Consciously bringing awareness to your breath and focusing on how you breathe can positively impact your nervous system and break that cycle.

MINDFUL EATING

Like breathing, you might think that eating is mostly a biological process for survival. And if you're on a desert island, it might be. But food is much more than calories and nutrients. Sometimes you may need to rush through meals or "grab-and-go" on the way to work, school, or other activities because you only have so much time. Preparing and eating food is something done so many times a day that it can seem like it's taking over your life, especially with kids. But when you barely taste the food you're inhaling to prop up your blood sugar or make up for a rough day, it can contribute to stress and anxiety, gastrointestinal problems, and poor sleep.

Mindful eating has nothing to do with the type of food you eat; rather, it has everything to do with how you approach eating it. When you find small ways to slow down and tune in, it can have a strong impact on your physical and mental health.

The Benefits of Mindfulness

It can be hard to imagine the benefits of mindfulness in your everyday life if you feel like you're in constant survival mode. You're already trying to conserve brain power, energy, and executive function to get through the day. But when you're racing through so many moments of your life, you're also missing out on experiencing them. This isn't to make you feel guilty, but is just to point out how easy it is to fall into this trap.

Becoming a parent provides a great opportunity for more presence since you have to tune into your baby's needs. Kids interrupt your ability to run on autopilot since they throw off your habits and rhythms. When you consciously stay present and tuned in, even for short periods of time, these interruptions can feel less stressful and your physical and mental health can improve over time.

LIVE IN THE PRESENT

Children naturally live in the present moment with little awareness of time passing. Think of your baby, just a few months old, engrossed in watching the breeze move the leaves of a tree, or the reflection of a sunbeam on the wall.

By the time you're an adult, you struggle to do what came so easily as a child. You're taught that you need to be busy and productive at all times. Even when you're doing something, you're thinking about what's next, what impact your actions will have, and even the consequences of doing (or not doing) them.

This has a huge impact on parenting when you worry about how your child's current behaviors will look in the future instead of focusing on what they need in this moment to build connection and resilience. Working on your own ability to stay present can improve your ability to respond instead of react and meet your child where they are.

MANAGE STRESS AND ANXIETY

Emotions are physical, physiological responses to feelings and stimuli. You feel emotions in your body and then perceive them with your mind. You can't deal with feelings effectively if you don't let yourself notice and sit with them. When you let them bottle up, it increases your stress level, and before you know it, you've entered that cycle of stress and shallow breathing. Just noticing and being aware of your feelings helps immensely.

RELEASE JUDGMENT AND FEAR

Everyone has an inner voice that is made up of the internalized messages you've learned, implicitly or explicitly, throughout your life. And while its job is to keep you "safe," your inner voice often tries to do so through criticism and judgment, which can often be more harmful than it is helpful. It might say things like the following:

"What will people think?"

"What kind of person does that?"

"Who are you to disagree?"

It's easy to listen to that voice! But mindfulness can help you notice when that voice comes up and if what it says is actually true. If you aren't aware that your inner voice is speaking to you from a place of fear, you might unknowingly listen to it instead of being present and aware of what is actually happening right now and what you need in this moment. Increasing your awareness of that inner voice (the kinds of messages it sends you and when) allows you more opportunities to respond rather than react to stressful situations.

DEVELOP GREATER SELF-COMPASSION AND SELF-LOVE

In her book *Compassion and Wisdom in Psychotherapy*, Dr. Kristin Neff explains that "self-compassion entails being warm and understanding toward ourselves when we suffer, fail, or feel inadequate, rather than ignoring our pain or flagellating ourselves with self-criticism."

Most people start their parenting journey wanting to be "good parents." That sounds reasonable, doesn't it? But when you break it down, if you don't do all the things that you think "good parents" do, the alternative in that binary is that you might believe you are a "bad parent."

There is a lot of gray area between those two options. When you're constantly presented with staged images of "ideal parenthood" on social media, it's easy to compare yourself to a curated and edited vision of daily life.

What if you allow yourself the space to be imperfect and know you're doing the best that you can in each moment? How does that change your thoughts? And what does that model for your kids?

IMPROVE SELF-ESTEEM AND SELF-CONFIDENCE

The "good/bad parent" binary can also wreak havoc on parents' self-confidence. There's no "one right way" to parent, no matter how many books and articles you read, and you won't know if you're making the "right" choices for years. However, there is so much information about parenting these days that it can seem like you're one misstep away from ruining your child forever. Luckily that isn't true, but it can cause anxiety for many parents who are trying to parent "the right way." That's an admirable goal, but parenting also requires flexibility to deal with the current moment.

Mindfulness can help you focus on making the right choice right now, which can help you feel more confident in your abilities to be aligned with your values for your family.

SUPPORT THE IMMUNE SYSTEM

Stress creates a physiological reaction in the body that impacts your heart rate and breathing. Controlling your breath can reduce your heart rate and blood pressure almost immediately.

In addition, mindfulness practices also positively impact the immune system. Studies published in *Annals of Family Medicine* and *Annals of the New York Academy of Sciences* have looked at illnesses ranging from respiratory infections to HIV and seen benefits from meditation. Since mindfulness can also reduce pain and stress and improve sleep, there is a positive impact on the immune system from those factors as well.

The Challenges of Mindfulness

There is so much messaging passed along in early childhood (and beyond) that is not mindfulness-based. You're often encouraged to "push through," "keep it together," and "put on a happy face."

You're also likely taught to be busy and productive at all times, so having a still body or a still mind is something you don't often experience without guilt. If you've been bottling things up for years, you may have a lot of old feelings and experiences to sort through. If you do manage to slow down, not having a distraction from strong feelings can be a new, uncomfortable sensation.

LEARNING TO SIT WITH YOURSELF IS HARD

When someone is upset, most people's first instinct is either to cheer them up or distract them. (This also goes for yourself.) Are you likely to jump through flaming hoops and contort yourself into knots to avoid feeling uncomfortable? After training yourself to be constantly on the go and always *doing* something, just *being* is extremely hard.

Do you feel guilty if you're not busy with something all the time? Do you feel like you need to "earn" rest or relaxation? If so, it can help to remind yourself that taking even a few minutes for mindfulness can help you be more productive.

If you don't have an external focus, you are able to notice other things, like your feelings, your thoughts, and your physical sensations. The good news is that you don't have to sit there very long to see benefits, and you can only improve from here!

DIFFICULT EMOTIONS, FEELINGS, AND MEMORIES MAY COME UP

Everyone has a unique combination of personal history, neurology, and physical experience that makes mindfulness easier for some people than others. Mindfulness can be a particular challenge if you have a history of trauma or were raised in an environment where feelings were discouraged or if you're neurodiverse and/or anxious and struggle to identify your feelings. Just because it's difficult doesn't mean it's impossible or a waste of time, however. You just need to find an approach that works for you.

Sometimes the fear of confronting feelings you've avoided for a long time can be overwhelming, and if you have anxiety or trauma, working through some of that with a therapist may be necessary. For most though, it's awkward, uncomfortable, and temporary. Feelings aren't forever.

THE MIND LIKES TO WANDER

If you tend to fall into the category of "perfectionist," mindfulness may seem challenging because there's not a "right" way to do it. It's common to have people sit down, try to clear their mind, and just seconds later announce that they have failed because a thought popped up.

Of course it did! Your brain doesn't stop thinking just because you're sitting still. Thoughts will still float around: your physical sensations, that itch on your knee, the item you forgot to get at the grocery store . . .

That's not doing it wrong; that's just part of the process. The fact that you noticed a thought is what mindfulness is about. The ideas that come up provide an opportunity to acknowledge and accept those distractions and return to your body and your breath. It means you're doing it right.

DESIRE TO MULTITASK

Contrary to popular belief, humans are actually terrible at multitasking. There is the belief that it's faster or more efficient, but adjusting your focus from one task to another actually makes each task take longer than if you did them one at a time. Of course, some situations might demand it, but the more you can focus on a single activity, the better you can perform it.

STRUGGLING WITH MINDFULNESS? THESE TIPS CAN HELP

TIP #1
Plan Ahead and Schedule It

It's easy to start the day thinking, "Pfft, I'll be able to squeeze in 5 minutes for mindfulness." Then you blink twice and find yourself a zombie at 10 p.m. The brain's resistance to change and new activities is an old survival mechanism that's intended to prevent you from eating poisonous berries or falling off a cliff. (This is also why your toddler is a stage-5 clinger. Smart!)

This survival mechanism is less helpful when it's triggered by something you *want* to do but are subconsciously resisting. Instead, make a specific plan for when you think some mindfulness practice is most likely to work. Think of it like a science experiment; if it doesn't work, then you have more information so you can try again. Does your little one sleep in? Choose something to try as soon as you wake up. (Check out chapter 10 for time-specific ideas.) If you're blearily up with a bright-eyed toddler before the sun, maybe their naptime or after bed would be better.

Give Yourself a Gold Star

What motivates you? Are you intrinsically motivated and just need to know how mindfulness will help? Or do you need to bribe yourself a little bit? Would tracking meditation minutes excite you (you could make a graph!) or cause you anxiety? Do you struggle to start things, or to keep going with them? Do you do better alone or with a buddy?

The "best" way to incorporate mindfulness into your life is in a way that actually works for you. If you're able to push the limits of your comfort zone, that's amazing! If not, start where you can. You know yourself best. Do what you can and adjust as needed.

TIP #3

Listen to Your Heart

Some people may be nervous about starting a mindfulness practice because they're worried about what will happen if they stop distracting themselves from their feelings. If it's a new experience, it's normal to feel resistance.

Something that can help is reminding yourself that you're safe, and you can stop at any time. If something becomes too intense or causes anxiety, you can simply stop. Part of mindfulness is paying attention to what thoughts and sensations come up, and that might include learning your limits.

Mindfulness is all about being present for whatever activity it is that you're doing that moment. When you're so used to switching rapidly between tasks, it can feel slow when you don't. Think about a moment of recent multitasking. What would it have been like to focus on a single activity at a time instead?

THE GLORIFICATION OF BEING BUSY

Capitalist culture glorifies being busy and productive. Sitting around is seen as being lazy. It's supposed to show commitment to work through your lunch break and never take time off. But then when it's time to slow down, you may struggle because of those internalized messages. Your productivity does not determine your value as a person. You are worthy of rest and do not have to earn it.

Even people who talk about health, self-care, and relaxation often frame it as a way to recharge so that you can work more efficiently once you've rested. When you focus on the values you want to live, you can be more intentional about your choices.

Many people feel the need to grab a snack or their phone just to fill free time since being still can provoke anxiety. This is especially true for people with ADHD.

CONSTANT OVERSTIMULATION

Along with staying busy and constantly multitasking, you are also likely to be constantly bombarded with all kinds of sensory and media input, such as piped in music, appliances, pinging phone notifications, airplanes flying overhead, the television on as background noise, traffic, sirens, and landscaping sounds.

You may be so used to it that you barely notice anymore, but it's another situation you process on autopilot. When you get still and quiet and listen to what is going on with you, a whole host of things will likely pop up that you didn't notice before. This takes practice and will likely feel strange at the beginning. But the more you practice acceptance and self-compassion with whatever feelings arise, the more you might find you enjoy the silence.

Building a Consistent Practice Takes Time

It's hard to do new things and learn new skills. Practicing is frustrating and hard. And that's what happens when you're new to using mindfulness. It's not peaceful or easy at first when you feel like you're wrestling your own brain into submission, then realize that you were thinking about trying not to think, and feel like you've failed.

It's okay to start small. You can read articles and studies about maximizing the results of your mindfulness practice and testimonials that claim the "best" way is to meditate for 45 minutes every day at 5 a.m. on a mountaintop while facing east and wearing a red scarf. Or you can just take a breath when you remember and build from there.

In a stressful moment, a few breaths can have an impact in under two minutes. Bigger picture, you're re-teaching your body how to react to stressors, building those skills, and modeling them for your kids so they can learn to co-regulate themselves. It's a long-game strategy.

The Power of Five Minutes

Sure, maybe 45 minutes would be better, but that can feel impossible when you're being pulled 17 different ways already. It's okay to start one breath at a time, even if it takes a while to get to just 5 minutes of focus a day.

It's easy to assume that mindfulness is a synonym for meditation and that you must get set up and sit on a pillow in silence, but any moment can be a mindful one with the right approach.

How long does it take to make coffee or tea in the morning? If you have an electric kettle or automatic coffee maker, you can take those minutes to tune in while your beverage brews. If not, see the "Tea-Time for the Soul" practice in chapter 9 (page 136) for a simple ritual to mindfully drink it.

Lather, rinse, repeat, meditate? A nice soaking bath would be great, but what about squeezing some extra mindfulness into your shower or skincare routine?

Maybe you have a capsule wardrobe and one child, or you're like me with three kids and a Laundry Mountain with regular seismic activity. There's plenty of advice to fold laundry while watching TV or fitting in a podcast, but what if you turned off the media sometimes and actually slowed down some chores that can feel tedious? They have to get done anyway, so instead of folding while zoning out, you can tune in and double-dip with some self-care.

HOW WILL I KNOW IF MINDFULNESS IS MAKING A DIFFERENCE?

Valid question! Chances are good that if you're making an attempt, you're doing it "right." Signs you may notice after you start your practice include the following:

- Increased patience when frustrated

- Less body tension, including fewer headaches or back pain

- Better sleep (either falling asleep or staying that way)

- Improved observation of nonverbal communication

- Reduced anxiety and perseveration

- Fewer instances of "spinning brain"

- Increased capacity for empathy

- Improved communication and ability to listen

- More focus and fewer distractions

Many of these are related. If you've been impatient with people because you can't fall asleep due to stress, and your mindfulness practice reduces your stress levels, that allows you to fall asleep, and more rest allows you to be more patient. Increased patience allows you to be more present and empathetic with your toddler, which can improve communication and reduce stress for both of you. It's a win-win!

Some changes are gradual or subtle, so it may not seem like much until one day you realize that you're more calm and able to manage daily stress more effectively. Take it one day, one moment, one breath at a time.

Key Takeaways

That was a lot of information, but the good news is that there's no quiz. Mindfulness is not any one specific activity or technique; it's simply the process of paying attention to the present moment. The practice of mindfulness is rooted in ancient spiritual traditions and is incorporated in many faiths; or can be entirely secular (and is presented that way in this book). Popularized in the United States by Jon Kabat-Zinn and his Mindfulness-Based Stress Reduction program in the 1970s, mindful meditation is just one approach of many. A mindfulness practice has many observed physical and mental benefits, regardless of which modality you prefer or why you are starting.

- There's no "right" or "wrong" way to practice mindfulness, and some is better than none. Meditation, visualization, breathwork, gentle movement, mindful eating, and other methods are all valid. The important thing is to practice.

- Mindfulness can have both mental and physical benefits. Reduced stress, better sleep, lower blood pressure, improved communication, increased patience, and more restful sleep are all possibilities. It can also increase self-compassion, self-confidence, and self-esteem, help you stay present, and reduce anxiety and judgment.

- You're conditioned from a young age to stay busy and "productive," and avoid strong feelings, so sitting with your thoughts and emotions can be difficult and uncomfortable at first.

- Mindfulness isn't a magic solution where you can "be mindful harder" and see immediate results. But if you keep coming back to the practice and find even a few mindful moments a day, you'll get benefits.

- Five minutes doesn't sound very long, but even committing to that brief period can have a disproportionate impact. If you can sit and zone out for a TV episode, you can squeeze in five minutes that will improve your physical and mental health!

Now that you have a foundation in what mindfulness is and how it can help, let's talk about those amazing toddlers, shall we?

2

Mindfulness for Raising Toddlers

oddlerhood can be the most fun, exciting, hilarious, and terrifying stage of your little one's life. They're delightful and dramatic, and you can almost see their minds develop like a time-lapse video of a blooming flower. On the other hand, your previously sweet baby can turn into a stubborn, screaming disaster in the blink of an eye due to the alignment of the stars and phase of the moon.

It's easy to get caught up in the maelstrom if you don't have tools and strategies for yourself, and mindfulness is a powerful one. Being able to hold space for your child and focus on the present is a huge gift for both of you. Finding ways to help yourself stay calm, manage your own triggers, and support your child can be very hard in the moment. A mindfulness practice makes a solid foundation for you to fall back on when your child needs you to help them co-regulate.

Toddlerhood Is an Exciting Time

Toddlerhood can be one of the most fun stages your kids will ever reach. They're still babies in many ways, but they're growing so fast you can literally see it happen. Their unique personalities start to shine through, but you're still their world, and they're still snuggly and small. After more than a year of adjusting to a new family dynamic, this parenting thing isn't quite so new either.

But with your little one's development comes new challenges. Babies' needs can be intense, but toddlers have new, big feelings that cannot be contained in their bodies. Your baby learns to say "No," which can also provoke big feelings for you. Every child develops skills on their own timeline, so it can start to feel like your child is "behind" other kids. Everyone has their own strengths and challenges, including adults.

Just remember that every parenting journey is unique and contains many moments of conflicting feelings. You can be grateful for your toddler, love them to the moon and back, and also feel resentful and stressed about how challenging it can be. There are no "bad" feelings for either of you, and by modeling a full expression of emotions and how to handle them, you're helping your child learn.

It's Also a Time of Transition and Change

Toddlers are mobile. They're starting to talk. They're getting opinions. And they are not always happy about it. You need a whole new approach to parenting as they get smarter every single day. Literally. Toddlers develop more than one million neural connections per second! Can you imagine how busy their brains are?

Toddlers become scientists and explorers as they learn about the world. They develop strong preferences, a sense of independence, and new ways of communication. Sometimes it feels like you can't blink without them getting into (or onto) something.

Along with fun developmental milestones like better communication, other new behaviors aren't as exciting. The intensity of their feelings about bananas may have you doubting every choice you've ever made. Is getting the wrong cup truly the end of the world? It might be. They liked something this morning but hated it in the afternoon. Maybe it's the full moon, or just molars coming in.

The sweeter baby days fading can be bittersweet. Even though watching them grow is exciting, it's also hard to keep up. They don't even know what they want, so how can you? It's frustrating to feel like you can't win.

CHANGE CAN BRING FEAR AND WORRY

Along with delight and frustration, this transition can cause stress. It's normal to worry about your child when you're unsure about their growth curve, when they aren't sleeping well, or they take a tumble on the playground. New behaviors can trigger unexpected strong emotions.

If you find that you're experiencing a level of stress or anxiety that's interfering with your daily life, or feel like you're just going through the motions, I encourage you to seek some additional help. The Resources section at the end of the book provides more information on postpartum mental health services.

Parents of young kids have many possible sources of stress. Mindfulness can't prevent the source of stress, but it can be a tool for better managing it.

How Mindfulness Can Help

You've probably gathered a lot of parenting advice along the way. You know what you're supposed to do, but when the time comes, that advice is much harder to implement in the moment. You also know how mindfulness can physically and mentally impact you, but where do those benefits overlap with parenting a toddler?

If you've heard of the "80/20 rule," it applies to parenting as well. Only about 20 percent of parenting is about what your kids do; 80 percent is how you react or respond to it. According to all the books, you must stay calm and hold space. But that is easier said than done.

This is where mindfulness comes in. There are many reasons why it's hard to stay calm when your sweet little one does their loudest impression of an emergency siren in the middle of the grocery store, and that's what this chapter is about.

BE PRESENT, LISTEN, AND LEARN

Many parenting worries are not actual emergencies, but small issues that compound throughout the day until you're convinced your child will have a horrible future because they don't want to share their new truck at the park.

There's nothing wrong with imagining your child's future (yes, they are clearly a rainbow xylophone prodigy destined for Juilliard!), but most minor incidents are developmentally appropriate. When you get trapped in those catastrophizing thoughts, you're worried about the future. If you can stay in the moment, you can figure out what's actually going on, not just what you think is going wrong. Mindfulness helps you notice patterns and adjust accordingly. Your child isn't mean; they're just worried the other child won't return their toy.

SEE THE WORLD THROUGH YOUR CHILD'S EYES

Kids are incredibly mindful and present. There's a reason for the phrases "childlike wonder" and "beginner's mind." Children involved in play are fully immersed in the task at hand and have little grasp on the abstract concept of time until near school age. They don't rush, and they often struggle to transition between activities.

Adults would be better off following their lead. When adults transition between activities it's called "task switching," and we're not good at it. Schedules crammed with work and errands and activities force you to keep thinking of what's happening next instead of what's happening now. You miss opportunities to let the journey be the destination. Slow down. Stick to one task at a time. Stay present. Children can be great teachers if you let them!

FIND PEACE WITH HOW YOU WERE PARENTED

Parenting may be your life's biggest personal development project. No matter what your upbringing, becoming a parent can give you greater appreciation for your own caregivers, or gain a new perspective on their actions. You may want to emulate your own parents, or you may be breaking cycles of generational trauma.

Even so, if you don't have a plan on how to respond in moments of stress, you will probably revert to what your caregivers did when you were a child–whether that's what you want to do or not. Staying present with an upset toddler is hard. How might your caregivers have acted with access to the same information you have? You don't need to forgive someone who harmed you, but you may gain new understanding.

ADDRESS YOUR PARENTING TRIGGERS

Parenting triggers are events or cues that subconsciously activate a physiological response from the past. They could be from trauma, but even if you had a relatively idyllic childhood, you may still experience triggers from growing up. You may not even be aware of them until your child does something small that provokes a disproportionate reaction from you.

Common triggers include whining, crying, "talking back," taking risks, wasting food, having big feelings, being noisy, being messy, arguing, hitting, or not listening. When your child does one of these things, you don't respond calmly but react based on the way you felt as a child when your brain sent a "danger" signal.

If you can identify those trigger behaviors and discover what's underneath, you can learn to calm yourself and respond how you want to.

MANAGE STRESS, WORRY, AND FEAR

Toddlers are still relatively new to the world, but they seem so much older than babies. Their new behaviors and developing personalities can cause stress for caregivers, however. This is often the flip side of parenting triggers. Instead of a response from the past, these fears are usually about the future.

What if my child doesn't learn to make friends? What if my child never talks? What if they can't play a sport that I love? What if . . .

There is a tendency to catastrophize minor incidents and assume that how things are today is how they'll be forever. But if you sit with that feeling, it isn't true. Staying with your child in the moment allows you to meet them where they are and reduce your fears and worries about the future.

RELEASE GUILT AND SHAME

What makes you feel guilty as a parent? Maybe it's working, not working, breastfeeding, not breastfeeding, co-sleeping, not co-sleeping—you get the idea. No matter what you do, someone will say you're doing it wrong.

There are so many variables to consider: where you live, what your profession is, if you have family support or not, if you or your children are disabled or neurodiverse, etc. Based on those factors, you must make the best decisions you can for you and your family. Your options are different if you went back to work right away compared to someone with paid leave and extended family nearby.

You're doing the best you can with the resources available. You can't solve systemic problems by yourself.

STOP COMPARING YOURSELF TO OTHERS

Social media is a mixed blessing for parents. Any advice you might need is at your fingertips any time of day, but you're also inundated with images of perfect families in coordinated outfits having fun when you're struggling to fall asleep at night.

But when you're focused on what other families are doing, you're not focused on what your family needs. What works for them might not work for you. Parents often see posts online and think that they need to do more, but filling your schedule with activities is too much for most toddlers–and adults.

Let yourself slow down and think about what you enjoy, not just what you think you're supposed to do with your kids. Be more *you*.

STAY CALM AND PROBLEM SOLVE

Staying calm is one of the hardest parts of having kids. You're tired, you're stressed, you're triggered, and suddenly you're yelling when you didn't mean to. This is where mindfulness can have a huge impact. A regular practice can improve sleep and reduce stress so you're less reactive. New calming strategies to stay present allow you to breathe through strong feelings and get to the root of the problem instead of reacting out of fear.

When you or your child are in fight-or-flight mode, your amygdala rules your brain. You literally can't think logically when you're primed for survival. The power to stay calm lets you help your child co-regulate, then solve the problem together.

CONNECT TO YOURSELF AND YOUR CHILD

Part of mindfulness is accepting what is happening in the present moment. A big trap of parenting is having unreasonable expectations of what it will look like, and then feeling resentful that it's harder or more time consuming than planned.

If you can manage those expectations and show up just as you are, then allow the same for your child. For example, instead of feeling frustrated that they aren't asleep yet, release that expectation and need for control and just be there. Noticing those feelings helps you get recentered, and then you model how to manage your emotions for your child.

FEEL EMPOWERED AS A PARENT

Toddler behaviors can provoke many strong reactions, especially when they start using the word "no." Many adults weren't allowed to tell their parents no, so your child doing this may automatically sound defiant or disrespectful to you. Their burgeoning independence can trigger you since they're harder to control.

Trying to control them just adds to frustration on both sides since it doesn't work. When you can tune into where your reaction is coming from and adjust to respond from a feeling of calm presence, you're better able to parent the way you want. No one is at their best when they're triggered.

PRACTICING MINDFULNESS WHILE PARENTING A TODDLER

You might assume that a mindfulness practice needs to be done alone, and it certainly can be done on your own. But, as the parent of a toddler, it also may be difficult to imagine even five minutes uninterrupted when you can't even go to the bathroom by yourself.

The reality is that your toddler has a constant presence in your life, and they can be part of your mindfulness practice, too. So much suffering comes from resisting what is, but there are some simple ways to not only accept but also incorporate your toddler into your practice.

Narrate what you're doing. Children absorb everything from spoken language to where you hide the good snacks, and when you grab your phone out of habit. Instead of scrolling mindlessly, tell your toddler, "I'm texting your grandparents the cute picture I took of you this morning." Say what you're walking into the kitchen to get. That builds language for them, and awareness for both of you.

Observe your child at play. When toddlers can immerse themselves in an activity, they're incredibly present and mindful. Watch and learn from them! It can be tempting to think that faster development is somehow better, but meet your child where they are and really look at what they're doing. Notice if the urge to interject praise comes up and see how it feels.

Model calming and co-regulation. Children need to see others calm themselves so they can learn this skill, too. Tell them, "I'm going to take some deep breaths. Do you want to join me?"

How to Develop a Lasting Mindfulness Practice

The hardest part of developing a practice is starting one. The goal is to create a practice that lasts so you have strategies that benefit you for the long term. You only need a few minutes a day to begin, and once you've built a habit, you can go from there. Ideally, you'll have a quiet space, at least to start. Then decide what you want to get out of this practice and if you have any specific goals.

Some people may love a particular modality where others may need to mix up methods to keep things fresh and interesting. What's important is that it works for you and helps you achieve your goals. The next hardest step is staying the course. Part of being mindful is noticing when you're judging yourself. If you miss a few days, it's harder to start again, but it's a beautiful opportunity to recommit.

COMMIT TO FIVE MINUTES PER DAY

A mindfulness practice is like compounding interest—the more you put in, the more you get out. Most people do best starting small and building a foundation from there, and it gets easier, like strengthening a muscle.

Jon Kabat-Zinn's MBSR course involved 45-minute daily meditation sessions. While that sounds peaceful, those people probably didn't have toddlers. Instead, commit to spending just five minutes per day on mindfulness.

What time works best for you? If you wake up before your kids, early morning might help set the tone for your day. If you're a night owl, go with that. Your lunch break? Naptime? In the car before you go into work? If you pick a time and it doesn't work, take that information, and try something else.

FIND A QUIET SPACE

When you're getting started, it's best to find a quiet place, or as quiet as possible for now. You already have your thoughts to contend with, so it's easier if you can avoid distractions. Some of the exercises are intended to be done anywhere, but try to make it as simple as you can at first.

This can be a challenge with a toddler at home, so consider your scheduling options, or even try noise-cancelling headphones or earplugs (they dampen sound, but you can still hear your child if they need you). Gradually, you should find that ambient noise fades into the background, or it can be something that you acknowledge and let go as a part of your practice.

SET AN INTENTION

Why mindfulness, and why now? How are you currently feeling? How do you want to feel? You don't need an earth-shaking event or reason but understanding where you're starting and where you want to go has an impact on your practice. Not only does it help you track your progress, but it can also keep you motivated and moving forward.

What's your intention for your five-minute practice? Maybe it's to stay centered or be more present with your child. Maybe it's to break the cycle of trauma and create a strong connection with your toddler. Maybe it's to improve your and your child's ability to co-regulate. There's no wrong answer, and it may change as you progress. What's important is that it resonates with you.

TRY NEW PRACTICES

You may be tempted to try something familiar, or just one type of exercise. That's a great place to start! The danger is if that approach isn't a good fit right now or doesn't work for you, you could feel like you're "bad" at this. That's why so many options exist.

If one exercise is working well, try alternating with another type of practice. If something feels like a struggle, move on to something else. Some people are more visual and do best with something to look at or picture in their mind. Others may get distracted by the same. See how your body and mind respond to various types of practices.

MAKE NOTE OF WHICH PRACTICES WORK BEST FOR YOU

Not every practice will work for everyone, and that's fine. You're not failing if you struggle with some exercises; you just haven't found the best practice for you yet. Keep track of which exercises you're attracted to, which ones are easier, and which are more challenging. Do you do best when you're seated, or does movement work better?

Noticing how various approaches work for you is a mindfulness exercise of its own. Ask yourself what made a particular practice easier or harder for you. If one type is frustrating, set it aside for now and revisit it later to see if it's changed as your practice develops. It's all an experiment that gives you more information.

STICK WITH IT

Mindfulness isn't a quick fix, despite an almost immediate physiological impact, and has more benefits the longer you practice. How long will it take to see results, though?

In 2009, Phillippa Lally, a health psychology researcher at University College London, published a study in the *European Journal of Social Psychology* that found new habits take, on average, about 66 days to become automatic. With a young child at home, it's very easy to get sidetracked–by a rough night's sleep, an illness, etc. If you miss a day, don't give up. Can you squeeze in a few breaths tonight? Notice how you feel and commit to five minutes the next time. Keep showing up for yourself.

STAY OPEN, AWARE, AND JUDGMENT-FREE

The goal of mindfulness isn't to sit still or empty your mind; it's simply to be present and open to the process, tune into your mind and body, and observe yourself without judgment. Everyone has an internal voice that can encourage or criticize. What would it feel like to acknowledge that voice, but then let it go?

You may doubt that you're "doing it right." You may be more distracted some days than others, but so long as you show up for yourself, you're on the right track. If you need to shift your body, notice and acknowledge it. If you're feeling anxious, tune into where you feel those sensations in your body. If you fall asleep, you must have needed the rest.

CREATE A SUPPORTIVE ENVIRONMENT

Just like there are a variety of mindfulness practices, there are many ways to set yourself up for success. None are necessary, but you might try some of these options.

Comfort. Most meditation recommends a seated position if possible, but if your body isn't comfortable, you'll be distracted. You can sit on a chair or couch, or on the floor with a pillow or blanket to raise your hips higher than your knees.

Ambience. It can help to create a tranquil environment for your practice. You may enjoy lighting a candle. A favorite essential oil in a diffuser is another way to add aromatherapy.

Journal. Keep a mindfulness journal: Note how long you spent and what you did, or reflect on the day's session. A written record of your improvement can add motivation.

Mindfulness Is a Gift

Life with a toddler can be exhilarating, but unpredictable. Mindfulness smooths over the inevitable bumps and turbulent moments by giving you some peace. When the day goes south, you'll have the tools to sit with yourself and notice what comes up instead of being critical. You can come back to your center after feeling overwhelmed or out of control. You'll also model to your little one that everyone has feelings, even grown-ups, and there are ways to calm yourself back down.

When you feel guilty and are trapped in your own head, you're not able to process and learn. Honoring and reconnecting with your physical sensations, thoughts, and feelings allows you to approach each situation with curiosity and awareness.

This shift in your perception doesn't only apply to challenging situations; you may also find more moments of joy and connection.

Think of your practice as a compass to keep you oriented on your journey through parenthood. No matter how lost you feel, you can count on your compass to guide you in the right direction.

It Starts with You

When all your energy constantly goes to take care of others and there's none left for yourself, you can feel resentful. Making yourself a priority allows you to show up as the parent, partner, and person you want to be. Self-care has become a buzzword for buying yourself things, but it's really anything that improves your physical, mental, or emotional well-being. Mindfulness does all of that.

Your mindfulness strategies are a model for your kids, and so is what life looks like as a parent. Parents often think their kids want to spend more time with them, but if you ask kids, they really want their parents to be happy. Taking five minutes for yourself benefits your whole family.

Feeling overwhelmed and rushed probably isn't making anyone happier. If you're already stressed out, spending more time with your child in that state won't help. Focus instead on being present with them and make the time count. Mindfulness is a powerful tool to identify the circumstances when you feel particularly engulfed by feelings of guilt, resentment, or anger.

Key Takeaways

Toddlerhood can be a wild ride for everyone. Huge leaps in physical, mental, and emotional development are both exciting and frustrating. New behaviors or regressions in actions or sleep can reveal emotional triggers you didn't know you had. Operating from a fear that how something is now is how it will be in the future causes untold stress, just as reacting based on your past does. If you can focus on staying present with your child in the moment, you're better able to calm yourself and respond as the parent you want to be.

- Mindfulness can not only help reduce general stress but also have an impact during moments of frustration. You can improve your ability to notice how your body feels and what your triggers are so you can better manage them in the future. You can improve your connection with your child, understand your own background, and judge yourself less.

- It's normal to worry about your toddler since a good portion of your responsibility as a parent is to help keep them safe. If your concerns start to impact your daily life, you may want to get some additional support. Reach out to your preferred health care provider or see the Resources section at the end of the book for other options.

- A mindfulness practice isn't a panacea and won't change things overnight but sticking with it will pay off for you and your child many times over. Modeling a full range of emotions along with strategies to calm yourself down is a valuable experience for your child.

- You don't need to spend a lot of time or money to start a mindfulness practice. All you need to get started is a commitment and five minutes a day. You've got this.

PART II

5-MINUTE PRACTICES

You understand the types and benefits of mindfulness and have a plan to incorporate a few minutes per day into your life. So, what do you actually do for those five minutes?

In these chapters you'll find a range of mindfulness practices that focus on different aspects of life and incorporate unique perspectives. You might find that you are drawn to one method over another, or that your preferences shift as you practice. You'll be able to choose from relaxation techniques, prompts for self-reflective thought and writing, affirmations and mantras, and even some mindful art activities.

Each chapter focuses on one specific goal: clearing your mind, tuning into your body, breathing mindfully, staying calm, managing big feelings, connecting with your child, finding community support, improving your daily life, and using practices to start and end the day.

Many of the exercises can be practiced with your child. Remember that modeling even a few deep breaths can help your little one co-regulate, learn what to do when they experience intense emotions, and build a foundation for those skills as they grow.

3

Soothe Your Mind

Toddlers can push every button you have, and many you didn't even know existed. It can be unnerving to have such strong feelings toward a child you love so much. It can also be a challenge to focus entirely on or empathize with your child if you're distracted or anxious, but sometimes there are reasons you're distracted or anxious.

This chapter starts with some beginner-level meditations and includes tools and strategies to slow down your thoughts, stay present in the moment, and feel more centered so you're better able to handle the stresses of daily life. You will also see how to acknowledge and process your feelings, increase your capacity for self-love and self-compassion, and accept yourself on this journey.

One Mindful Minute

If you've never tried a meditation practice, or are feeling especially fidgety, start here. A little structure and guidance can help alleviate anxiety for some people, so this short, basic meditation is a great start. No matter how stressed you get, no matter how convinced you are that you don't have time, you can always come back to this 60-second exercise. Once you get through one minute, you can continue, but the smaller commitment can be easier to make.

1. Find a comfortable position, standing or seated, and set a timer for one minute.

2. Close your eyes, inhale through your nose, and exhale through your mouth at a normal rhythm. Notice how the air feels going in and coming out.

3. On each exhale, relax your shoulders. Feel gravity pull you down and the earth support you.

4. Breathe until the timer goes off.

Sunlight Meditation

Try this simple meditation when you're feeling overwhelmed. It's not complicated, and you can take five minutes to do it anywhere that it's safe to close your eyes. With an image to help you focus, you can control your breathing and clear your mind. You can set a timer for five minutes if it would help, but if that would distract you, just breathe on your own for as long as it feels comfortable.

1. If possible, sit upright in a comfortable position with your feet flat on the floor, shoulders and hands relaxed, or find a position that works for you.

2. Breathe normally for a few moments, focusing on how your breath feels going in and out of your body.

3. Make your exhales slightly longer to help deepen your breathing.

4. In your mind, picture a ball of warm, glowing sunlight, about the size of a marble. Imagine it entering your body through your navel.

5. As you inhale, visualize the ball of light getting brighter. As you exhale, imagine it getting bigger. As you breathe, watch it fill up your body, glowing like the sun.

6. Imagine that everywhere the light touches is bathed in that warm light, relaxing as it fills with the sun's rays.

Focused Doodles

You don't need to consider yourself artistic to doodle, and doodling can improve focus and recall when listening to information. This exercise combines a visual element with the sensory input of drawing to keep your attention focused on your task instead of your thoughts. A repeating pattern creates a rhythm that aligns your hand, eye, and mind to create a relaxation response in your body.

1. Get a pen and paper and sit somewhere comfortable.

2. Hold your pen and focus on the feel and weight of the pen in your hand. Adjust your grip and notice any changes.

3. Choose a shape and start drawing. Keep drawing the same shape (circles, squares, hearts, spirals, stars, loops, etc.) over and over.

4. If you feel uncomfortable or get tired, notice that sensation and reposition yourself. Draw for five minutes, or until you feel relaxed.

Coat Check Your Worries

Many parents find their priorities shift after having kids, and they worry about things they never even considered before. This can cause anxiety, especially concerns about the future or about what's out of your control. Some may be small issues that you don't know enough about yet, or a fresh news story about the latest reason we're doing everything wrong. This visualization isn't to invalidate your concerns; rather, it's intended to acknowledge them and tell yourself that you'll just worry about them another time.

1. Find a comfortable place to sit or try this in bed before you go to sleep.

2. Close your eyes and picture yourself traveling down a path in a peaceful forest. The sunlight is warm on your skin, and the ground is solid beneath you.

3. As you move forward, birds sing, and a stream babbles in the distance. You approach a clearing, and a gleaming gate appears before you. Next to the gate is an enormous tree.

4. Picture all of your worries, every concern big and small, floating out of your body and forming spheres. They are all different sizes and colors.

5. One by one, you take each sphere, acknowledge it, and say, "Thank you for keeping me safe." Then hang it from a low branch on the huge tree.

6. When you're finished, know that your worries will be there when you're ready. You turn away from the tree and approach the gate. It swings open to reveal a beautiful garden. You enter the garden feeling safe, supported, and at peace.

Brain Dump

Toddlers are unpredictable, so frequent interruptions are common. This can lead to many unfinished tasks and projects that take up valuable mental space. Thoughts of what you need to do may even keep you up at night, worried that you'll forget something important. You may have lists scattered around the house, but then you have to remember where they are. When you get all those thoughts out of your head and create an external list, it can clear out some mental space and allow you to be more present. Try this weekly and see what frequency works best for you.

1. Get a pen and paper, open a digital document, or open a voice recording program, then find a comfortable place to be.

2. Record everything you're thinking or worried about, no matter how big or small. Don't think too hard about it or edit yourself.

3. Once you're done, go through the list and eliminate anything that you can't control. Be merciless.

4. Repeat again and note everything you don't need to do yourself.

5. For the last round, focus on what's left. Divide it into multi-step projects and short tasks. Put those in your calendar and breathe a little easier.

Heart Meditation

Sometimes the busy-ness of life can distract you from enjoying it. This meditation is to help you focus on one person, connection, or relationship. This could be your toddler, your partner, a family member, or a friend. Use this practice when you're feeling resentful or disconnected.

1. Sit upright in a comfortable position with your feet flat on the floor, shoulders and hands relaxed, and eyes closed. If that's not accessible, you may want to recline, lay flat, or stand with your knees softened.

2. Breathe normally for a few moments, focusing on how your breath feels going in and out of your body.

3. Place one hand on your heart and make your breaths a little longer.

4. As you inhale, picture a spark lighting up your heart. On each inhale, see it glow a bit brighter until it turns into a beam of light.

5. Picture the beam of light aiming at someone you love, surrounding their body with a glowing halo. Keep beaming the light from your heart and let the image of their body absorb that love until their heart glows, too.

Box Breathing

Box breathing is a rhythmic breath pattern that helps soothe the mind and body. It's easy to remember, which makes it perfect for those days when you're tired and want to squeeze in a mindful moment. Some people find it helpful to use their finger to trace on a surface or in the air to add a small amount of movement. Experiment and see what works best for you.

Once you're comfortable with the breathing pattern, play with adding a mantra to each step. Suggestions follow each step but are entirely optional.

If at any point you feel lightheaded, dizzy, or anxious, discontinue the activity. Check with your health care practitioner if you have lung or breathing issues.

1. Find a comfortable seated or standing position and imagine a square.

2. Trace one side of the square as you inhale for a count of four. Mantra: "I breathe in gratitude."

3. Trace the next side of the square as you hold that breath for four counts. Mantra: "I am full of life."

4. As you trace the third side of the square, exhale for four counts. Mantra: "I release that which no longer serves me."

5. Trace the last side of the square as you pause for four counts. Mantra: "I am calm."

6. Repeat this sequence three to four times.

Strengthen Self-Compassion

When your mind feels like a tangled mess, writing your way out of it can be constructive. This isn't about creating a polished product; rather, it gives your mind a way to process your thoughts outside of your head. The physical act of writing is a powerful tool, though you can type it out if that's easier.

People are usually their own biggest critics and say to themselves things they would never say to another person. How can you reframe that? Because this exercise focuses on one issue at a time, you can use the same questions when new challenges arise.

1. Get a notebook or journal and pen, open a document on your computer or phone, or use a voice recording program.

2. Write or speak about the following prompts:

   A. What feels like your biggest challenge or struggle right now? How do you feel when you think about it?

   B. Consider your response, then imagine a friend came to you and told you those were their struggles. What advice would you give them?

   C. Where are you being unkind to yourself? What do you need to hear instead?

Accepting All Feelings

You may criticize yourself for being distracted while meditating and try to ignore any thoughts that come up, but the goal isn't to empty your mind; it's to notice your thoughts without judgment. Simple, but not easy. Similarly, when you get frustrated or impatient with your toddler, you may judge yourself a bad parent. The idea that every moment should be happy is a form of toxic positivity that doesn't leave room for the full breadth of experiences in life.

Instead of chastising yourself when you're not living up to your own standards, acknowledge and accept those thoughts. It's not pretending the critical thoughts don't exist, it's just noticing they're there, and letting them pass by.

1. Notice when you're having a judgmental thought, such as "I'm a terrible parent" or "I should be able to handle this."

2. Pause for a moment and name what you're feeling. For example, you might say, "I'm feeling powerless and angry." This lets you acknowledge how you feel instead of pushing it down.

3. Try to locate tension in your body, then direct your breath to that area. You likely won't entirely accept these feelings right away, and that's okay. Aim to accept a little more each time.

Moving Meditation

If sitting still is challenging or uncomfortable, or you just want to mix up your practice, a walking meditation is one alternative. Incorporating movement and changing up your environment can add a fresh perspective and be helpful for people who struggle to focus consistently. If walking isn't an option for you, consider another physical movement that *is* accessible where you can focus on breaking down each part of the motion. Listening to your body is a mindfulness exercise itself.

If you walk frequently, it may seem strange to break down something as familiar as taking a step, but we rarely notice automatic movements like that. A walking meditation can be practiced inside or outside, but make sure you're in a safe place so you can concentrate on your practice.

1. Find a place to walk, indoors or outdoors, where you have a clear path. You can use part of a longer walk as your meditation, or just walk back and forth at home if that's what's available.

2. As you take each step, notice the components of the movement: lift the foot, move the foot slightly ahead of your body, place the foot on the ground, and your weight shifts forward as the back heel lifts.

3. Take 10 to 15 steps, paying attention to each one, at a slow pace, then stop and breathe for several mindful breaths before walking again.

4. When your attention inevitably wanders, simply acknowledge it and return your focus to your body.

Clear Your Mind by Coloring

Your little one may not be coloring yet, but you certainly can. Like doodling, coloring combines a visual focus with small, repetitive physical movements to help create a whole-body experience. Coloring is a great activity if you need to feel like you're *doing* something. There are a multitude of adult coloring books available. You can also download and print coloring pages or use a kid's coloring book (with or without your child).

1. Find a coloring page or book to your liking. You're more likely to stick with it if you like the design.

2. Choose a medium: colored pencils, crayons, or markers.

3. Find a supportive place to sit, or lay on your stomach on the floor.

4. Begin to color. As you do, notice how the writing utensil feels in your hand, how it feels to use varying amounts of pressure, and even how coloring sounds and smells.

5. Color for at least five minutes, or until you feel more focused and relaxed.

Take Off Your Crabby Pants

This one is a little silly, but it works. Just like putting on a uniform or formalwear can change how you feel, taking it off again can, too. When you're feeling particularly irritable, give it a try. It's a combination of gentle movement, in a way, and a sort of affirmation to give yourself an emotional do-over. It's especially effective if you're wearing less comfortable clothes and can change into loungewear. It's not meant to ignore the feelings, but to accept them, then consciously choose another way.

1. Notice when you're feeling edgy or grumpy and acknowledge it either to yourself or out loud to your child.

2. Tell yourself (or them) you must have put on your "crabby pants" by accident, and that's why you're in a bad mood. You can also decide what type of pants to put on instead.

3. Go and physically change into another pair of pants or other clothes. Call them your "happy pants," or your "silly pants," or whatever feels right.

4. Notice any changes in your mood or level of patience.

MAKING THE MOST OF MEDITATION

There are millions of "right" ways to meditate, so part of a new practice is paying attention to what works and what doesn't work for you.

- Do you prefer being still, or moving?

- Do you prefer silence, or does music help you relax?

- Can you comfortably sit on the floor, or do you prefer standing or lying down?

You may want to repeat one practice to see your progress, or you may prefer to rotate through several options. Which appeals more to you?

Meet yourself where you are and make your practice your own. If you love to journal and write, do that. If you love to be in nature, do that. If exercise is your meditation, do that.

4

Check In with Your Body

C ortisol, the stress hormone, can negatively impact brain function, and can also build up in the rest of your body. Repeated exposure can reduce blood flow and increase lactic acid buildup in your muscles, prolonging muscle tension. Your shoulders and lower back probably knew that already.

Physical discomfort can create a cycle of tension and increased stress, neither of which helps you be a calm, centered, responsive parent. You may have been taught to "push through" pain or ignore it, along with your feelings, which can make it harder to connect with physical responses. When you bring your attention back to your body, you can better understand how you feel physically and emotionally. You can locate where you hold your tension and address it, often reduce pain, feel more grounded and strong and make peace with your body and all it does for you.

Be gentle with yourself. This can bring up mixed feelings, particularly for people socialized as girls. It's hard to connect to your physical self when you're taught implicitly and explicitly that your body is "bad," shameful, or wrong. All bodies are "good" bodies, including yours!

Your Body of Work

Your body is your home. Your body is the only one you've got. Everyday you are peppered with messages that tell you to buy products, programs, and potions to change your body into something else, but your body is already doing incredible work. If you have trauma in this area, or a physical disability, some additional support for this exercise may help. You know yourself best.

1. This is more powerful when written down, so get your journaling supplies and find a quiet place.

2. Write a letter to your body thanking it for all that it does for you. It grew up and survived puberty. It has grown and/or comforted your child. Notice when you feel some resistance or hear dissent from your inner critic.

3. Save the letter somewhere that you can read it when you need a boost.

Direct Your Breath

Your breath impacts everything from your digestion to how you use your muscles. This exercise helps you increase awareness of how you're breathing.

1. Tie a resistance band or thin scarf around your ribs at the base of your breastbone. It should be snug enough to stay put without feeling restrictive.

2. Find a comfortable seat or lie down and breathe normally for about one minute. Notice where you feel your breath.

3. Direct the breath into the side ribs where the strap is. Try not to deepen your breath, just shift it.

4. After another minute, shift the same volume of breath into your back ribs, using the strap to feel where your ribs expand.

5. After approximately a minute, try to use that same volume of breath to expand your ribs evenly into the strap all the way around. Do this for a minute or so.

6. Remove the strap and observe how your breath feels.

Complete the Stress Cycle

Your ancient ancestors faced different stressors than you do in modern life, but your body hasn't entirely caught up. Your amygdala doesn't care if you're facing a tiger or an upset baby (which is why it's almost physically painful to hear your baby crying in the car). You might intellectually know that a threat has passed, but your body stores that information until it gets a firm "all clear" message.

Here's how you can convince your body that a threat has passed.

1. Lie in bed on your back.

2. Start with your feet and tense them as hard as you can for a slow count of ten, then relax and breathe. Move up to your calves, thighs, buttocks, etc., and follow the tense-and-release pattern.

3. Repeat, or spend a longer count on areas you hold a lot of tension, like your neck and shoulders. You may feel a shivering or shaking sensation, especially in those extra-tense muscles.

4. For added catharsis, try the visualization Amelia and Emily Nagoski suggest in their incredible book *Burnout*: "Visualize, really clearly and viscerally, what it feels like to beat the living daylights out of whatever stressor you've encountered."

Build Your Own Sensory Nest

You probably learned the five senses as a kid, but did you know there are actually eight? Some people need more sensory input, others need less. The right amount of sensory input can be incredibly relaxing, but if you're disconnected from your body, you may not realize what changes would help.

You may use some of these items to help soothe yourself already; this activity just has you collect them in one place. Nothing needs to be purchased unless you want to, and the list is only some ideas to get you thinking.

1. Collect items that appeal to each of your senses. Keep them together to create a sensory "nest" area, or a toolkit. There are suggestions below, but use what you have on hand or what works best for you. Everyone's sensory preferences are unique.

   Sight: an eye mask or a dark room to reduce visual input

   Smell: a scented candle, a bottle of room spray, or a small bottle of essential oils with a scent you love

   Taste: gum or mints, carbonated water, or ice

   Touch: a soft blanket, fuzzy pillow, or stress balls to squeeze

   Sound: noise-cancelling headphones, earplugs, or relaxing music

Proprioception (where your body is in space): a beanbag chair, a nest of pillows or couch cushions, a hammock, or a weighted blanket for deep pressure

Vestibular (your body's orientation): a swing, a rocking chair, or a couch or other object from which you can hang upside down to invert your body

Interoception (your sense of internal body cues): a glass of water or a snack (or go to the bathroom)

2. When your body is feeling tense or overstimulated, take a few breaths and notice where the tension is and what you might need.

Wave of Peace

You probably carry tension in your body without even noticing. It builds up, your body compensates to avoid pain, and you get used to it. Bring some awareness to areas of tension to help you relax and restore.

1. Lie in bed or on a yoga mat or blanket on the floor if that's comfortable.

2. Focus on your toes as you breathe normally. If possible, gently move your toes to bring extra awareness. Next, move your focus to your feet, and work your way up your body to your head. Notice any places that feel tight or tense.

3. Send your awareness back to your toes. Close your eyes if they aren't already and visualize a gentle ocean wave ebbing and flowing. Picture the wave coming up higher each time you inhale, eventually reaching your toes. As you exhale, picture the wave rushing away, taking all tension from your toes with it.

4. Continue to visualize the wave washing over your body, inch by inch, washing away all the tension as you breathe out. When it reaches your head, it just goes softly around your face, pulling away any tension from your jaw, forehead, even your ears.

5. Check in with your body. You can end there or picture the wave working its way back down to your toes if you still feel some tension.

Track Your Heart Rate

This exercise can be particularly helpful if you have a hard time gauging how your body feels. Starting with data can increase your awareness so you can advance to less-structured activities more easily.

1. Find a heart rate monitor, see if you have one on your smartphone, use a pulse oximeter, or take your pulse by manually counting your heartbeats for 60 seconds (see the Resources section, page 157).

2. Next time you're feeling frustrated, anxious, or upset, check in with your body. Does it feel like your heart is racing? Check your pulse.

3. Now focus on your breathing for at least 60 seconds. Breathe into the tense places in your body and relax on the exhale.

4. Check your pulse again. Has it changed? How does your body feel?

Blow Bubbles

Joy and pleasure can only be experienced in the moment, so if you're continually distracted or anxious, you can't be present for those feelings of happiness. By adulthood, most of us don't have (or make) time to play. Having a child gives you the opportunity to play again, which is the perfect time to be more mindful.

Blowing bubbles is a simple pleasure, and the act of forcing out air can help deepen your breathing. To prevent a mess, this is ideally done outside. You can make your own bubble solution, or it's fairly inexpensive to purchase.

1. Grab some bubble solution and a bubble wand or use dish soap and a pipe cleaner shaped into a circle with a handle.

2. Find an open area. Enjoy this practice on your own or delight your little one (and any other kids nearby, since bubbles are irresistible).

3. Blow bubbles slowly or quickly, aimed high or low, and into the wind or sideways. How big a bubble can you blow? How many small bubbles? How high can they go before they pop? Really support your breath from your belly as you exhale.

4. Check in with yourself. Do you feel happier? More relaxed? If your little one was with you, what did you see through their eyes?

Body Scan Meditation

Being a parent can create major physical wear and tear, from potentially birthing a child to sitting on the floor to play or attempting to buckle an uncooperative toddler into a car seat. Everyday movements, repetitive motions, and awkward sleeping positions can exacerbate discomfort and pain, yet it may be so gradual that you don't notice.

Regular body scans can improve sleep, reduce muscle tension, and increase body awareness. You can practice it multiple times a day, or it's easy to sneak in before bed since it's best done lying down. Worst-case scenario? You fall asleep.

1. Lie down in a comfortable position; in bed is great.

2. Breathe normally and notice your breath. When you feel ready, deepen your breathing. You should feel your belly rise and fall.

3. Shift your attention down to your feet. Notice any sensation, tension, or pain. Acknowledge it and any thoughts or emotions that accompany it as you breathe into the tension.

4. As you exhale, imagine any discomfort leaving your body with your breath.

5. When you're ready, move up to your ankles and repeat the process. Move up your legs, torso, shoulders, and neck, all the way to the top of your head.

6. Notice where you hold tension and how your body felt before and after the scan. Repeat regularly.

Mindful Eating

Food isn't just fuel; it's culture, tradition, and memory. Society also likes to assign a moral value to "good" and "bad" foods, and pass judgment based on food choices. Plenty of people eat meals at their desks at work, or in front of another screen, barely noticing what they're eating until it's gone. After kids, you may be grabbing snacks on the run, or inhaling your food before it's their bathtime and bedtime.

A mindful approach to food slows you down to fully experience your food, whether it's a vending machine cookie, fancy pastry, or fun-size candy bar.

1. Engaging multiple senses helps you stay present. Look at your food before you start eating and notice how it smells. Can you pick out specific ingredients or spices?

2. Take a small bite of the food and appreciate the texture and flavor of it. Is it smooth, sandy, creamy, or crisp? Sweet, sour, or salty?

3. Chew the food until it's completely broken down. If you're just starting, aim for about 30 times. Don't take another bite until you've chewed and swallowed the previous one.

4. In a perfect world, you would continue this practice until you finish your meal, but you may not have that much time. Thích Nhất Hạnh advises, "Make the first bite a mindful bite." Start with the first bite and build from there.

Small Pleasures Practice

Pleasure can sound like a dirty word when you're constantly told that every moment should be productive. You probably miss small moments of pleasure while constantly thinking ahead; it takes you out of the present moment and keeps you in autopilot mode.

Instead, focus on those small moments of enjoyment. It could be snuggling into your favorite pajamas, curling up with your little one to read a story, the smell of your favorite shampoo, or a beautiful flower spotted near a parking lot. Collect those moments like treasures as you tune into the world.

1. Throughout the day, notice when you experience pleasure. It might be the perfect sip of coffee, a square of chocolate, new socks, a warm sunbeam, or playing with a family pet.

2. When you do, close your eyes, and give yourself a few breaths to sit with that feeling.

3. Take it a step further and take a photo or write in your journal about these moments.

Get Grounded

Anxiety can make you feel like you're trapped in the chaos of your own mind. Your body may feel out of control if your brain is frantic. Grounding techniques get you back into your body so you feel centered and calmer, allowing you to focus and be present again. Try this version, and adjust it based on what works best for you. If standing doesn't work for you, try sitting with your feet on the floor, or lying down.

1. Stand with your feet planted shoulder width apart. If possible, being barefoot will give you more immediate sensory feedback.

2. Press each toe into the ground and notice the floor holding you up and pushing back against your feet. Feel gravity pressing you down against the earth.

3. Close your eyes and visualize roots reaching down from the soles of your feet into the earth, connecting you and supporting you. Feel the earth's strength holding you, solid and firm.

Just Add Water

The power and versatility of water makes for accessible ways to bring yourself back to your body when you need to relax or re-center. The physical impact is almost immediate, and it's especially useful if visualization alone is harder for you.

Try this approach when you're feeling ungrounded and distracted, fidgety, or restless. Notice what changes. Try one step at a time or do whichever is most accessible at the moment. Adjust the temperature for comfort.

1. Acknowledge how you feel, and accept that it's not good or bad; it just is.

2. Take a sip of cool water. Feel the water in your mouth, as it goes down your throat, and through your body. Feel it wash away any disquiet.

3. Put your hands and wrists under cool running water. Imagine your stress being rinsed off and carried away.

4. If that's not enough, take a warm shower. Close your eyes and feel the water on your skin as anxiety and worry ooze out of your pores and are washed away.

5. Or, take a warm bath. Submerge yourself as much as you can and feel the stress soaking out of you into the water.

BODY POSITIVITY

Many people have a complex relationship with their body image. This can be true whether you've birthed a baby in the last few years, live with a physical disability, or have internalized messages from society about body faults and flaws. The point of these practices isn't to pretend all your thoughts are sunshine and rainbows; rather, the goal is to direct mindful loving-kindness toward your physical form.

Most of the marketing messages you get are about what's wrong with your body and how you should change it. How can you show your body gratitude in its current state?

What do you want your child to learn from you about their body, which may look like yours?

5

Keep Your Cool

Remember that list of things you said you would *never* do as a parent, back before you had kids? Are you done laughing yet? Imaginary children listen, sleep, and brush their teeth without argument. Real children, with their unique temperaments and personalities, tend to make life a bit more challenging.

Expectations of parenting don't always match reality. The greater the difference, the greater the frustration that things aren't going how they "should." You may feel powerless or out of control when, try as you might, you can't *make* anyone eat, sleep, or use the bathroom. The feeling of powerlessness can manifest as anger to cover the fear, and it's impossible to stay calm when you see that your toddler just tossed a giant jar of sequins all over the living room carpet like confetti (true story).

Luckily, mindfulness can help you keep your cool, even under pressure. The practices in this chapter will help you manage this season of transitions and change. You will learn to deal with worries, fears, and thoughts about the future. Make peace with the unknown, practice releasing the need for control, and accept that you don't have to have all the answers.

Mindfulness and Meltdowns

The intensity of toddler feelings can trigger a fight-or-flight response in you, and those instinct-driven parts of your brain can see your tiny person as a threat. You can't help them calm down if you can't calm yourself down.

Even harder, your child is melting down in public where your focus is split among your child, your own reaction, and the reactions of others. Staying present is challenging to say the least but gets easier with practice.

1. Check in with how your body feels.

2. Get down on your child's level to help you focus on them. If it helps, imagine your eyes as a camera zooming in on them.

3. Notice your breath. Is it shallow or fast? Feel your ribcage expand as you inhale, and the air rushing out as you exhale.

4. Resist the urge to reason with a crying toddler, as their brain is literally incapable of it while stressed. Continue to breathe to avoid being swept up in your own reaction. Imagine yourself as a rock, unmoved by a storm.

5. In a calm, low voice, say, "I'm here. You're safe."

6. If you feel yourself looking around, feeling uncomfortable, or tension in your body, come back to your child and your breath. You've got this.

Affirmations for Parenting

In challenging moments, it can be helpful to think of positive thoughts and your capacity to do well. These affirming phrases are useful reminders of your priorities during tense moments when you need a push to stay present.

No phrase will work for all situations, so here are some options to choose from. Post them where you can see them or test them out one at a time and see what resonates with you.

1. When you feel yourself getting impatient or reactive, pause and take a breath.

2. In your head or out loud, say the affirmation of your choice. Breathe. Repeat as many times as needed.

   - I am in charge of being calm no matter how my child behaves.

   - I am willing to learn and grow.

   - I have patience when I need it most.

   - I give my child the attention they deserve.

   - I take time to care for my own needs, which makes me a better parent.

   - I validate my child's feelings.

   - I am patient and understanding.

Vagus Nerve Stimulation

Both psychological and physiological responses are associated with emotions. Part of mindfulness is accepting those emotions in order to minimize the physiological reactions. You can also change physical input to affect those reactions, and thus your emotions.

The vagus nerve starts in the brain and stretches all the way down into the abdomen. It controls sensory, taste, oral motor, and parasympathetic (breathing and heart rate) functions of the body. Deep breathing impacts the vagus nerve to calm the nervous system and reduce your heart rate. When deep breathing isn't enough, you can stimulate the vagus nerve more directly to calm your nervous system and literally keep cool.

You can use this practice when you feel anxious, but you can also add it regularly to help calm your nervous system and reduce reactivity. Here are three variations that impact your vagus nerve.

1. Choose one of the following:

   • Splash your face with cold water.

   • Put an ice pack or bag of ice on your chest.

   • Take a cold shower for as long as you can stand it without shivering.

2. Notice how you feel before, during, and after applying cold.

3. If desired, track how long you can stand the cold and see if it lengthens over time.

Proactive Prevention

A number of these exercises focus on what to do when you're already stressed or anxious, but the most effective method is practicing when you're not already fighting yourself to keep calm and making time for strategies that reduce stress. More awareness of what energizes or drains you can have a significant impact and offer insight to promote more mindful time management.

1. Get a pen and paper, open a digital document, or open a voice recording program, and find a comfortable place to be.

2. Make a list of the things you always say: "I wish I had time to _____ . . ." or "I should schedule _____ . . ." For example: I wish I had time to exercise. I should schedule a massage. I should schedule lunch with a friend. I wish I had time to read.

3. When you're done (you can always go back and add more later), go through the list and make note of the activities that excite you the most.

4. Go to your calendar and make the time. Schedule some activities, call and make the appointment, text a friend, or whatever else you need to do. A plan alleviates anxiety and gives you something to look forward to.

Grown-Up Time-Out

Just as the phrase "calm down" has never once in history helped anyone do so, sending a child to a time-out to think about what they've done only gives them the opportunity to feel victimized and hurt. For adults, however, consciously removing yourself from a triggering situation can give you an opportunity to check in with yourself and adjust your approach while your child is safe.

You don't want to run on autopilot but having a plan can help you remove some decision-making in a moment of stress so you can focus on re-centering yourself.

1. Choose a location in your home where you can sit that is easily accessible. This will be your "safe spot."

2. When you're feeling triggered or are losing your cool, move your body to your safe spot and sit down. You can tell your child, "I need a moment to calm my body down."

3. Notice your body where it contacts with the seat. Notice your breath. Notice how you feel.

4. Repeat to yourself, "I am safe. I am loved. I am loving."

5. Check in with your body and continue until you're feeling calm.

Alternate Nostril Breathing

This breathing technique comes from yoga and is shown to reduce stress and anxiety. The first few times you may need to focus more on the physical technique, and that's okay. Acknowledge and accept that you're learning.

1. Sit in a comfortable position with your left hand on your left knee.

2. Place your right hand near your nose.

3. Exhale deeply, then use your right thumb to press your right nostril closed.

4. Inhale through your left nostril, then press the left nostril closed with your fingers as you release the other side.

5. Exhale through the right nostril.

6. Inhale through the right nostril, and then press it closed again.

7. Release the left nostril and exhale through the left side.

8. Repeat for up to 5 minutes, then complete the practice by exhaling out the left nostril and release.

The Manual Reboot

You've probably seen some memes where kids have dumped an entire bag of flour on the floor or poured pancake syrup on the dog. They're funny until you walk into a room and face a surprise yourself.

If you find yourself reacting with anger, most likely that anger is directed at yourself ("How could I have left them alone for 10 seconds to make such a mess?"), even if it comes out at your child. Instead, you can pause, take a moment, and start again. Manually reboot your system, if you will. Practicing this helps you handle unexpected situations more easily when you can avoid a knee-jerk reaction.

1. When you see a disastrous mess, simply freeze. If you open your mouth, close it again.

2. Focus on your breath. Did you gasp? Did your breathing get shallow? Close your eyes, or turn around if you can, to block out the scene while you regroup.

3. Notice any tension in your body and breathe into those areas. Notice the thoughts going through your mind, acknowledge them, and let them pass.

4. When you're able, open your eyes or turn back around to take in the scene again. Take another mindful breath, if needed, and make a plan to clean up.

Know Your Triggers

Emotional triggers are situations that you react to automatically based on past experiences. As parents, common triggers include your child being an age you were when trauma occurred, your child doing activities you weren't allowed to do, or your child behaving or expressing themself in ways you were punished for. You may not realize they exist until you have a strong reaction to something small.

The first step is to identify your triggers so you can be aware of them and be mindful of how you react. If they are trauma-based, you may need support from a professional as well.

1. You can do this in your head, but it's more powerful when you write it down. You can also look back and identify possible patterns.

2. Think of when you've had an immediate, strong reaction to something your child said or did (usually anger or anxiety). What happened before you reacted?

3. Close your eyes and think of the situation and how you felt. Where was that feeling located in your body?

4. Can you think of another time you felt that way? What was going on?

5. How do you wish you had reacted? What can you do differently next time?

Visualize the Future

Have you told yourself that you "should" parent a certain way? More patience, more special time, more activities, more books, whatever it is? Saying you "should" do something, then not doing it, is setting yourself up for self-judgment.

Instead, what do you *want* to do? Whether that's how you want to react in a situation, or what activities you want to plan, think of that. When you visualize things going the way you want, it's easier to break it down into steps and make it happen.

1. Decide what you want to do: respond calmly, plan an outing, etc.

2. Find a comfortable seat and close your eyes.

3. In your mind, picture the situation you chose. Like a movie, watch yourself react the way you want, step-by-step, seeing each detail and moment.

4. Next time that situation arises, breathe and remember what it looked like to play out that event.

It's a Catastrophe!

Every parent has vicarious hopes and fear-based visions of their child's future. When you take a current situation and project the outcome into the future, your reaction is about the slippery slope of possibility, not the situation (and child) in front of you.

Instead of letting your fears run wild, you can intentionally acknowledge your thoughts and follow them to their imaginary catastrophic end.

If you've experienced trauma, proceed with caution and appropriate support. Your fears may be based on your own childhood, even if your child is unlikely to experience the same thing.

1. Choose a situation or behavior that has triggered or frustrated you, then frame it as, "If they do X now, then they'll Y." (Example: "If they won't eat broccoli today, then they'll never eat vegetables.")

2. Continue creating "if/then" scenarios to continue down the slippery slope. (Example: "If they never eat vegetables, then they'll have nutritional deficiencies. If they have nutritional deficiencies, then they'll get sick. If they get sick . . .").

3. Follow this train of thought, no matter how absurd or illogical it may be, until you get to the total catastrophe. Usually this involves being unloved and alone.

4. Pause to breathe and notice any emotions or physical sensations that have come up.

5. Connect your original "if" to your last "then." (Example: "If they won't eat broccoli today, then they'll end up unloved and alone.")

6. Acknowledge and accept feelings that arise and notice how you feel when you consider your final if/then statement.

Mindful Discipline

One of the biggest shifts from parenting an infant to a toddler is the need for discipline. Unfortunately, the term is often associated with punishment or a need to stop certain behaviors. But discipline means "to teach," and though toddlers seem huge compared to their infant selves, they're still very new to living. They need to know what TO do instead of what NOT to do, and they need guidance, not punishment.

Adults know that "making lunch" involves multiple steps. Toddlers, with a dodgy grasp of time, do not–unless you tell them. If you can allow more time and keep them involved, you're teaching them important life lessons.

1. When you start a household chore that isn't time sensitive, tell your toddler what you're doing and what the steps are.

2. If they're able to participate, let them. Toddlers love to help!

3. Repeat each step as you reach it. "First, we will _____, and next we will _____."

4. Keep your instructions positive. "Please keep the water in the sink" is more effective than "Don't splash!"

Great Expectations

You don't wake up each morning planning to run out of patience with your little one, and they don't plan to make your life harder. But it can feel that way some days. The issue is rarely with them, and usually with adult expectations. When your expectations are too high, you'll be frustrated and stressed when they're not met.

In his book *The Explosive Child*, psychologist and author Dr. Ross Greene uses the phrase, "Kids do well when they can." When your toddler looks you straight in the eye and throws food or toys, they're not being malicious, they're acting like toddlers. Assume good intentions from kids and adjust your expectations accordingly.

1. Next time you feel yourself getting frustrated with your toddler's actions, pause and breathe for a moment, then ask yourself, "What did I expect them to do, and how can I adjust?"

2. For example, if you want them to leave a fragile item alone, you may need to acknowledge that it's too much to expect them to do that, and you need to move the fragile item to keep it safe.

3. If you find yourself thinking, "They should be able to do that," adjust your thought to "They can't do that yet."

GROUND CONTROL, DO YOU COPY?

Toddlers seem to be magnetically attracted to everything you don't want them to have, and they're fast. On the occasions they succeed in making a mess, even if you seem upset with them, you're most likely upset with yourself.

You are the only person you can control. Inconvenient as it may be, you cannot *make* your child do much of anything. You have a lot of control over their environment, so the only things toddlers can control are if they eat, if they sleep, and if they go to the bathroom. Avoid engaging in power struggles over these, because everyone loses.

Remember that your child's behavior is not an indicator of your value or success as a parent, only of what they can handle in that moment.

6

Make Peace with Complicated Emotions

You've probably heard some well-intentioned advice along the lines of, "Cherish every moment! It goes fast and you'll miss these days!" You may have mumbled a generic agreement and hurried away because you do not, in fact, cherish every moment of your child crying over the banana they asked for, and bedtime does not always come soon enough.

All your feelings are valid and none are bad. There can be pressure to pretend that everything is great, but if you can sit with the full range of your emotions, you can better understand yourself and your needs.

This chapter considers those complex, sometimes con-flicting feelings to give you a different perspective of why they might come up. Some of the feelings like perfectionism, shame, and grief can be intense. If you have trauma in your background, please proceed with caution. If a practice causes anxiety or is too much for you, try something else. The goal of these practices isn't to transform past pain in just 5 minutes; rather, it's to build awareness and think about where certain reactions may come from.

Being Okay with Being Okay

It's common for parents to hide their feelings in front of their kids, especially strong emotions. It's justified by saying that they want to protect their kids from those feelings. But children are extremely perceptive, and they learn so much by watching. That includes watching emotionally mature people show and manage their own feelings, even intense ones. It's also why you might sometimes hear your own parent's voice come out of your mouth.

Many parents also feel that they shouldn't admit to any mistakes since it would be a sign of weakness. Seeing adults make mistakes, accept responsibility, and then try again sends a much stronger message than putting up a facade of perfection.

It can feel very vulnerable to express yourself or admit error in front of others. Perfection is a myth. It's okay to just be okay.

1. Find a comfortable seated position and close your eyes. Breathe normally, paying attention to your body as you inhale and exhale.

2. After 5 to 10 breaths, think about an area where you're struggling as a parent and are being hard on yourself. Notice what feelings come up without judgment.

3. Breathe with these feelings for a few moments, then say to yourself, "I accept that I am doing the best that I can right now, and that's good enough. I am only human."

4. Observe any feelings or resistance that arise with curiosity. Repeat the statement, if desired, as you continue to breathe.

Body Mapping

Mindful practices can help you improve awareness of your body, but intense feelings can make it challenging to stay present. Body mapping is a technique used to think about the sensation of emotions in your body when you're not actively feeling those things. A physical representation of your feelings can act as a personal "cheat sheet" when you need it.

A larger version takes more time but can be a powerful art exercise. A simplified version as part of a regular journaling practice can track possible patterns or triggers.

1. Draw or print out the outline of a human body. It doesn't need to be detailed, just give the basic shape for reference.

2. Think of a situation where you had difficulty managing your feelings. Close your eyes and remember how your body felt in that moment. Breathe as you notice where the sensations are in your body.

3. When you're ready, open your eyes and draw what you felt on the body outline. There's no wrong way to do it; you might choose a color, a shape, or a pattern. Label the feeling if you want to name it, and use the same map multiple times, or do many single pages.

Strengthen Self-Compassion

Extending compassion to others can be much easier than giving yourself that same grace. Compassion requires the vulnerability to admit that everyone experiences hardship in some way, even if you don't like to admit that parenting can be a hardship.

What usually makes parenting so difficult isn't even your child's behavior but trying to get your child to comply with social norms. Give yourself a moment to acknowledge that some days are really hard, and that's part of life. Use this as a meditation, or as a time-out when you're struggling to stay calm.

1. Close your eyes and think of a moment that is causing stress or sit with the present moment. Observe how you feel.

2. Say to yourself, "I'm having a hard time," or "I'm feeling stressed and overwhelmed." Choose what feels correct at the moment.

3. Put your hands on your heart and breathe into your chest for a few breaths.

4. Now send yourself kindness, such as "I accept myself as I am. May I be patient. May I be strong."

5. Repeat as needed.

Green with Envy

It's common to feel envious of other people, whether it's people without kids or other families who seem to have it easier. You can feel guilty for having "negative" feelings about parenthood or others, or you can consider what those feelings can tell you. If you shove those feelings aside and judge yourself, they'll come back until you process them.

1. Use this as a self-reflection, or preferably a journaling prompt.

2. When you notice yourself feeling envious of someone else, be it in person or on social media, pause for a moment.

3. You might be tempted to criticize yourself, but sit with that feeling and ask yourself what about them do you envy? Do you perceive that their life is easier than yours? Do they have something you don't? Be specific.

4. Next, think about what steps you could take to have more of that in your life. When you have some ideas, how do you feel? Do they still feel possible or as attractive to you? Consider if it's under your control.

5. If so, write down some steps for you to move toward that goal. If not, breathe through those feelings, know it's okay to feel that way, and let them go.

Grieving Your Pre-Kid Life

Remember the days when you could just spontaneously make plans, or leave the house, or even travel at the last minute? Now it can be tough to get to the bathroom alone. You wouldn't trade your kids for the world, but that doesn't mean you can't miss the freedom of your life before they arrived.

It's normal to feel a sense of loss about your "old life," but guilt may prevent you from accepting and sitting with those feelings. This meditation can help you recognize that grief and treat yourself with compassion.

1. Find a comfortable seated position, close your eyes, and focus on your breath.

2. After a few cycles, deepen your inhale slightly and direct the air to your belly.

3. When you feel ready, visualize yourself before parenthood. Imagine you can talk to that version of yourself. What would you like to tell them? What would you like them to tell you? Imagine the conversation and listen without judgment.

4. When the conversation is over, thank your other self. Know that you can return to this space whenever you need it. Allow yourself to feel any feelings that come up and send yourself love and compassion.

5. Return your attention to your breath as you breathe normally.

Life Is Both/And

Guilt over conflicting emotions about parenthood is very common. When you express any feeling that's perceived as negative, many people think they're being positive when they attempt to remind you that it goes so fast and you'll miss these days. But, oftentimes, that feedback can feel invalidating and judgmental.

No one has only good moments and good days. You can feel both gratitude *and* frustration. You can feel both happiness *and* grief. You can contain multitudes.

1. Find a comfortable seated position and close your eyes. Inhale into your belly, and as you exhale, relax your face and shoulders. Repeat for 3 to 5 cycles.

2. Think of a feeling you've been judged for expressing, either by yourself or someone else. Hold that feeling, notice it in your body, acknowledge it, and accept it as it is. It's not good or bad; it's just a feeling.

3. Now think of a positive feeling you also have and notice how that feels in your body. Again, it's not good or bad; it simply is.

4. Next, hold both feelings at the same time and give yourself permission to do it. For example, say, "I can feel *both* tired *and* grateful for my child at the same time. I can feel *both* joy about my family *and* grief about my pre-kid lifestyle."

5. Breathe into those feelings and any tension that comes up and let them coexist.

Releasing Shame

Shame can be a heavy topic, and not one that can be fully addressed in a short meditation. The purpose of this practice isn't to sit for five minutes and come out healed on the other side; rather, it's to help you practice tuning into your body, and acknowledging thoughts instead of judging them. If the meditation brings up too much, simply release the prompts and return to your breath.

1. Find a comfortable seated position. Notice your normal breath pattern for a few inhales and exhales.

2. Slightly lengthen each inhale and exhale, breathe into your belly, and focus on your breath.

3. Gently redirect your mind to a moment when you felt shame, whether due to your own internal criticism or someone else's comments. Notice what thoughts and feelings arise around this memory.

4. Next, tune into any new sensations in your body: heat, pressure, buzzing, etc. Breathe into the sensations with curiosity.

5. This may feel intense and bring up a lot of feelings, and that's okay. Now tell yourself, "This feels uncomfortable and hard, but I am worthy, and I am safe." Repeat as needed.

6. Bring your focus back to your breath.

Values Meditation

Most information about toddlers centers on behavior—encouraging, preventing, and managing it. Of course, you want to foster positive behavior in your kids, but how often do you ask yourself why that is? So they avoid punishment? So you look good? So they grow up to treat others with kindness?

Though most parents would prioritize that last goal, there's likely a combination of all three involved. If you want to ensure that you're staying true to the values with which you want to raise your kids, you have to know what they are. It's wonderful to want to raise kids who are kind, but you need to know what that looks like, and think about how you model it yourself and how it plays out within your own family.

1. Find a comfortable seated position. As you close your eyes, notice your breath and any other sensations that arise. Observe them without judgment.

2. Give yourself a few minutes to stay there, breathe, and increase your awareness.

3. When you feel settled, ask yourself a few questions:

   A. What do I want my child to know?

   B. Are my actions in line with that value?

   C. What other actions would align with that value?

4. Sit with the answers, see what comes up, and notice what feelings accompany those thoughts.

5. Breathe for a few more cycles, then open your eyes.

6. Write down your thoughts if you find it helpful or think about your values when you approach parenting.

Positivity Practice

At the end of the day, it can be easy to rattle off a list of all the things that went wrong and didn't get done. There will always be more laundry and dishes and emails and items on the to-do list, though, and it can wear you down to constantly feel like you never accomplish anything.

But during the daily grind there are always bright spots, however brief and easy to forget they may be. When you tune into really noticing them, it can change your perspective considerably. Recording them gives your brain concrete evidence of that joy as a reminder that it's real.

1. Choose a time to reflect on your experiences each day. If you miss a day, get back to it the next day.

2. Write down three moments from the day that were positive, uplifting, funny, or otherwise noteworthy. This could be something your child said, a moment you shared, a message you received, or that you remembered your mindfulness practice that day.

3. It may be a challenge to think of three things, but a successful grocery store trip, remembering your umbrella, or drinking your coffee before it was cold are all valid options. As you build on this practice, you'll find you start to key into those moments during the day that you want to make sure you record.

Affirmations for Parenting

Parenting is a very long game. Doing it "right" won't stop your child from having big feelings, and you won't know how it turns out for a few decades. That can cause anyone to second-guess themselves.

In case you need a reminder that you're doing the best you can, try using affirmations when you're trapped in fears from the future about how your child will turn out.

Hang one or more phrases up where you can see them in the areas you spend the most time. Try saying them out loud in front of a mirror, or to yourself when you're trying to stay present and calm with your child. Choose one that resonates, rotate through them all, or modify one to suit your needs.

- I feel confident in my parenting choices.

- Connection, not correction.

- I model kindness to my child in my words and actions.

- We are both doing the best we can in this moment.

- This is the path I chose to walk.

YES Days

Toddlers hear the word "no" a lot. When they react to being told no, it's not because they didn't get "their way"; rather, it's because of the lack of control they have over their lives. Clearly you can't just hand over the car keys to your two-year-old because they want to go for a spin, but sometimes parents say no more from habit than actual necessity. It's not fun for anyone when a toddler loses it, so it's in everyone's best interest to prevent that.

Saying yes to a child can bring up some intense feelings, whether it's because your own family wouldn't (or couldn't) say yes to many of your requests or didn't spend much individual time with you. If it's safe, or a reasonable risk, why not? It can just be for five minutes, but a "yes day" sounds better.

1. Let your child know in advance you're planning a fun activity.

2. Explain the time frame to manage expectations (set a timer if needed), and that you might have to adapt to make things work. Then let them suggest activities or games. Make a list of ideas to use later.

3. Wherever possible, say yes to their ideas. If you can't, explain why and try to find an alternative. They may want to bake cookies, go to the park, read books, blow bubbles, or play with a favorite messy toy.

Scheduled Meltdowns

Sometimes you can tell that your child is on edge but can't quite let it out yet. A so-called "scheduled meltdown" can help them release the pressure of built-up feelings at a safe place and time (usually at home instead of daycare or school).

This concept works for adults, too. There are times when you may feel overwhelmed, but you still need to get through the day or week. Instead of trying to push those feelings down and building up more pressure, mindfulness techniques let you notice and acknowledge those feelings so you can manage them later.

1. When you're feeling anxious or overly stressed but don't have time to work through what you're feeling, stop what you're doing when possible, get to a safe place, and close your eyes.

2. Breathe into the tense places in your body and exhale that stress.

3. Notice those overwhelming feelings and sensations. Name them if you can. "I'm feeling anxious. I'm feeling over-whelmed. I'm feeling unappreciated."

4. Tell yourself, "I'm having a lot of feelings, but I'll worry about them later." Repeat until you feel more calm.

5. Later, when you *do* have time to process everything, consider ways to signal to both your body and your brain that you're now safe, and let those feelings out.

THE MYTH OF THE PERFECT PARENT

There's an idea that if you just read enough books, follow all the steps, and spend enough time with your child, you'll somehow attain Perfect Parent status. But it's impossible. Yet it has taken hold as a possibility that causes everyone to feel like they're failing.

Even if you're just aiming to be a "good parent," the only alternative is being a bad parent if you don't meet those standards.

- When you think about what a "good parent" does or looks like, what comes to mind?

- Think about the list of characteristics or actions. Is that even possible? Are those things you or your children want?

- What *are* you doing well? What parts of parenting do you enjoy most? How can you do more of that?

7

Connect with Your Toddler

Children are whole people with their own personalities, preferences, wants, and needs. Adults are really just grown-up toddlers who want to be heard and seen. You're also the model for your kids of how to treat others, and how others treat you.

Your children can be your greatest teachers, if you allow them to be. When their behavior triggers you, it's your reaction you need to manage, not their actions. In this chapter, you'll find mindfulness practices you can do with your child, ways to build empathy, and enjoyable ways to make time for connection. These small shifts can have a significant impact on your patience and your relationship.

Belly-to-Belly Breathing

Adults often have higher expectations of children than they do of themselves. If adults could manage their own feelings, there wouldn't be road rage, yet they want toddlers with only a few years of being alive to "self-soothe" when they're upset. But they can't.

What they *can* do is co-regulate: seek reassurance from a calm, responsive person who can model and help them understand their feelings. For this to work, you must be calm and responsive. When your little one is already upset, their brain can't reason, so you can't explain how to calm down. Modeling works for both of you since it helps you stay focused as well. Try this breathing exercise when your toddler is calm, then deploy it when they're struggling to regroup.

1. Lie down on your back, in bed or on the floor, or on a couch if there's enough space.

2. Position your toddler laying on top of you, belly-to-belly, holding them gently in place if needed.

3. Inhale into your belly so it rises and falls with your breath. Focus on making your breathing pattern as slow and even as possible. Though your little one may not be able to consciously take deep breaths, the goal is for them to unconsciously match their breaths to yours.

4. When they're calm, if they weren't already, you can say something like, "It helps my body feel calm when I take deep breaths like this."

Active Play

Playing together can help kids feel strong, burn off energy, and connect with you where you choose the amount of physical contact. It's also great for letting kids practice getting excited, then calming down again.

There are so many ways to play, so here are a few ideas to get you started. If this level of physical activity is too intense, consider other ways to let your child feel powerful and able to make choices, but in a safe environment.

Airplane: There are limited points of contact, but plenty of physical input for your child. Lay on your back, bend your legs up, hold their hands, and straighten your legs to "fly" your little one with your feet on their belly. Look into their eyes and focus on keeping them balanced.

Make a sandwich: Place a cushion or pillow on the floor and put your child on top, or have them climb on. Pretend to place sandwich toppings on them, the sillier the better. Spread on mayonnaise, or sprinkle on salt. Use a second cushion or pillow as the second piece of bread and "squish" the sandwich together before pretending to eat it.

Hide and seek: This is the best age for playing hide and seek because they usually tell you where they're going to hide, and you can hide under a blanket and get comfy. Win-win. Pretend you can't find them for as long as possible.

1. Suggest some ideas, but let your child choose the game. They learn to make decisions by making decisions.

2. Pay close attention to their reactions and adjust your actions accordingly.

3. Watch for signs of getting overexcited or tired and stop before they have a hard time calming back down.

The Six-Second Hug

Most people like hugs from those they love since they provide relaxing deep pressure and can stimulate the production of oxytocin, the "love hormone" that makes you feel good. A hug may seem pedestrian, but when you pay close attention to how long you hug, and how you talk about hugging, hugs can be a wonderful mindful practice.

Of course, you can give hugs often, but this approach is useful when your toddler is frustrated or upset. Giving them the choice to hug or not is subtle but important. Hugging also allows you to breathe and calm down before you respond.

1. When your child is frustrated and you feel your own body tensing up, notice your reaction and try to breathe into it.

2. Get down to your toddler's level and ask them if you can have a hug. If they say no, say, "Okay, when you're ready, I'm here."

3. Stay at their level, open your arms, and wait for them to come to you. Hug them for at least 6 to 10 seconds and continue breathing into the residual tension you feel.

Mindful Art Collaboration

Most toddlers are still working on their fine motor skills and hand-eye coordination, so their art is about process, not product, which is a perfect setup for mindfulness. When you join your child in their activities, you enter their world, and they feel more connected to you. Concentrating on a single project together keeps you both present and focused.

1. Suggest a joint art activity like coloring or painting or ask if you can join your child on something they are already at work on.

2. Work on a picture together or let your child play "art director" and give you instructions. This lets them feel a sense of control and allows them to use your mature motor skills to create their vision.

3. Focus on the feeling of coloring or painting and ask your child a few questions about why they chose a certain color.

4. Toddler attention spans typically only last a few minutes, so investing a short time can have a bigger impact than you might expect.

Tactile Sensory Play

Toddlers learn through experience since they have very little practice being in the world. That's easy to forget since they seem so much older and bigger than they were as babies, but they're incredibly new to life. As disgusting as it may seem to you, they touch and smell and lick things to get more sensory information to file away for later.

You have sensory needs as well; you just have more experiences filed away. Preferred sensory activities are very regulating to the nervous system, so they're a great opportunity to join your toddler.

Everyone has their own sensory preferences, so choose an activity that feels good to you and your child. The following are some ideas:

- Kneading dough, play dough, or clay

- Scooping and pouring rice, beans, sand, or water

- Playing with slime or water beads

- Sorting beads or buttons

1. Notice how your body feels before the activity. Is your mind racing? Are your shoulders or jaw tense? Do you feel anxious? Let your breath fill your body and expand those places.

2. As you participate in your chosen activity, focus on what you're doing and how your body feels. Do you notice any changes?

3. Also observe your little one as they play. What details do you notice that you might have overlooked?

Toddler-Paced Nature Walks

Toddlers love practicing and mastering new skills, and once they're walking, they often want to walk on their own, no matter how long it takes. This can be frustrating when you're trying to go somewhere or accomplish something. Seize this opportunity to practice exploring and mindfulness.

The key is that your goal isn't to *go anywhere* on your walk, just to be where you are. That might be to the end of the driveway or the end of the block. Let your child set the pace and choose the direction (within reason and safety, of course), then see the world through their eyes.

1. Invite your toddler on a walk. Let them know ahead of time if there's a time limit. (Make sure you're wearing appropriate clothing and shoes, and take some water along.)

2. Have your child decide which direction to take and head that way.

3. When they stop to point something out, stop and look. If possible, get down at their level to share their perspective, and ask what they see.

4. Between stops, notice how the sun or wind feel on your body, and how your feet feel on the ground. What do you see that you haven't detected before?

5. Give your child plenty of advance notice before it's time to head home.

Quotes for Connection

Toddlers' feelings can be intense, and so big that their bodies can scarcely contain them. These feelings range from understandable (having to leave a place when they're having fun) to rather mysterious (you handed them the cheese they asked for). Because their "big" problems can feel relatively small to adults, it may be hard to empathize with their upset in those moments. It's also a common inclination to want to "fix" or even stop strong emotions that aren't inherently negative.

A supportive phrase can remind you to deal with the child in front of you, not the one inside you who wasn't allowed to feel that way. Read them as needed, hang a list up on your fridge, or write them on sticky notes around the house. Whatever works.

- My responsibility is to hold space for feelings, not to fix them.

- It's not an emergency. No feeling is forever.

- It's healthy to express feelings.

- I can stay calm, not add to the chaos.

- Observe and breathe, then respond.

Cleaning with Kids

Sometimes the most frustrating phrase in the world is, "I want to do it myself!" Letting little ones "help" can feel like one step forward, two leaps back.

But isn't the goal of raising kids to teach them what they need to know for life? It's tempting to rush through cleanup or put it off until later so you can play with your child, but it's also an opportunity to connect with your toddler and teach them something. This isn't to suggest that you always include them but offering them a chance to feel useful and work toward mastery helps build their confidence and skill set. Instead of a task to rush through, chores can be something you do together.

1. Include cleanup as the last step of each activity, whether it's cooking, playing, or changing clothes.

2. Break each activity down into small steps for your child. If it requires them, try to have tools or a workspace their size or level (like having them wash dishes in a tub on the floor, or get a small broom).

3. Notice when you have the urge to take over from them. What do you feel in your body in those moments?

— Manage Interruptions Mindfully —

It's truly impressive how your child can be totally content until you're focused on something else, and it's like they have a primal need to interrupt you. It can also be exasperating, but there is an explanation.

First, toddlers are dependent on adults for their safety, so a distracted caregiver is perceived as a threat to their survival. Just realizing that can help you reframe their clinginess. Second, it's often a bid for connection. If your instinct is to shut them down to deter them, try this practice and see if it helps.

1. When possible, spend some time entirely focused on your child before you must leave or need to concentrate on something else. This could be a few minutes of snuggles, connection, or reading a book that can smooth the transition.

2. Remind yourself that it's not an emergency and no one is hurt and focus on your breathing.

3. If you get interrupted and you're stopped anyway, give them the attention they need for a few minutes. Join their world and stay there for a moment.

Mindful Praise

For years the parenting advice was to build up your child's self-esteem through praise. Now "participation trophy" is used as a pejorative. You have to tell your child when they're making good choices though, don't you?

Actually, no. You can acknowledge and celebrate accomplishments with your child, but praise tells them to look outside themselves for evaluation, and that they're only "good" if others tell them so. This might sound like a slippery slope, but if you're skeptical, try being more mindful about your reactions and see what happens.

1. When your child does something new or shows you something, notice your reaction. Are you proud? Happy? Tense?

2. Observe your child. What is their expression? Do they look to you for approval before showing their feelings?

3. When you say "Good job," ask yourself if you're saying it for your child's benefit, or your own need to comment.

4. When you feel compelled to praise, take a breath first and just observe. How does that feel in your body?

Right Now Is Not Forever

When a toddler throws a toy or hits someone, it's easy to think that they'll be this way forever. The same goes for co-sleeping or snuggling kids to sleep or any number of behaviors or comforts.

Just as birth weight is no indication of adult height, your child's behavior as a toddler is not a straight line to their behavior as an older child, teenager, or adult. Instead of projecting their current behavior into the future, picture the future and work backward to see the path.

1. Sit or lie down in a comfortable position and close your eyes. Focus on your breath until you feel centered.

2. Picture your child as they are now. Notice the details of their personality that give them their unique spark.

3. Take those details and imagine 20 years in the future. If tended and encouraged, what could that spark become? Imagine the best-case scenario of how your child has grown to adulthood.

4. Hold that image in your mind, and work backward, like a movie in reverse, to how they arrived there. What did that person learn from you to shape them? How does that make you feel?

Increasing Empathy

When your little one collapses on the floor because the water in their cup is too wet, it can be hard to take them seriously. But children have so little control over their lives and have such a limited scope of the world that small things feel much bigger to them. When you can't see from their perspective, it may seem silly, but when you can take their view and empathize, they'll feel seen and understood.

You may be naturally empathetic, or you may need more practice to improve. Start from wherever you are.

1. Find a comfortable seated position and close your eyes. Focus on your breath.

2. Think of a time when you were disappointed, or something didn't go as planned. Did you feel powerless? Frustrated? Angry? Sad? Hold those feelings and notice any sensations that come up in your body.

3. Breathe into those feelings and exhale the tension out with your breath.

4. Next time your child is upset about something seemingly small, remember how you felt in a parallel situation. What did you need to hear? Can you give that gift of understanding to your child in this moment?

PUT YOURSELF IN THEIR SHOES

If you struggle with empathy, try to reframe the situation in adult terms to imagine your own reaction. Examples include the following:

- Your toddler is crying because another child took their toy at the park. Someone said they need to learn to share.

- Someone took your car. You called the police to report it stolen.

- Your toddler is upset because you gave them the food they asked for and now they don't want it.

- Your restaurant meal contains an ingredient you don't like and didn't see listed. You don't want to eat it but you're hungry.

- Your toddler refuses to use a cup because it's the wrong color.

- The shirt you ordered arrived and it's the wrong color, so you don't want to wear it.

8

Look to Your Community

Modern parents may have more access to information than previous generations, but resources are not the same as physical and emotional support. Humans are social animals, even as personal needs for interaction vary, and you're meant to be part of a community. Whether it's from your extended family of origin, like-minded families, a professional support team, or others, you need encouragement and assistance. Many parenting resources make assumptions about what a family looks like or needs, so if your experience doesn't match that, it's vital to find a community who understands. That could be single parents, LGBTQ+ families, neurodiverse families, parents estranged from their family of origin, or other situations.

Community comes in many forms: in-person, online, reading materials, podcasts, and more. You deserve to be surrounded by love and respect, as do your children. At times you may think you've found the right group only to find that they're not the right fit, or you have conflicting beliefs or needs. Being more in tune with your needs and those of your child can push you to set boundaries, ask for what you need, and look for inspiration and encouragement.

Transform Suffering

Human instinct is to avoid pain, suffering, and negativity, yet they are part of the full human experience. Many meditations acknowledge negative feelings, but the Buddhist practice called tonglen ("giving and taking" or "sending and receiving") focuses on them. Using tonglen as inspiration, this meditation encourages you to transform suffering with your breath energy, like plants take in carbon dioxide and give off oxygen to clear the air.

You can't avoid suffering, and parenting is not always laughter and kisses. Sometimes just sitting with those feelings can be enough, but other times, the only way out is through. Try this on a tough day and know you're not alone.

1. Find a comfortable seated position and close your eyes.

2. Breathe normally for a few cycles and focus on your breathing.

3. Imagine all the difficult, frustrating, and tedious parts of parenting. Think of the late nights, challenging schedules, guilt, pressure, and giant messes. You can do this for just yourself, or all parents with the same stressors.

4. On your next inhale, breathe in all that suffering, of yourself and all those you're thinking of. Inhale with the intention of taking away that suffering.

5. On the exhale, breathe out love and peace for the same group. Imagine your breath spreading as wide as possible.

6. Repeat, breathing in as fully as possible, transforming that energy, and radiating out the positive energy to the world.

Ancestral Practices

Whether you lived in a multigenerational home, never met your grandparents, are a genealogy buff, or were adopted, there are ways to connect with your ancestors and offer them gratitude for their gifts. Your ancestors could be parents or grandparents, aunts or uncles, or even a mentor or teacher whose guidance you value even if you're not related.

Even those you didn't know or meet have passed something down to you. It might be genetic, a piece of family history or wisdom, an heirloom, or a story.

1. Many cultures have a practice of having a space to honor departed family members. If this includes you, you can sit near it, or simply picture your ancestors in your mind. If not, you may want to collect photos, keepsakes or heirlooms, or favorite items or foods of your ancestors.

2. Close your eyes and breathe as you picture your ancestors, as images if you have them, or as you imagine them. See them form a circle of support around you.

3. Tell them, "I am grateful for the gifts you've given me in body and in wisdom."

4. Breathe in gratitude and wisdom, breathe out solitude.

Forgiveness Meditation

Parenting your children can bring up strong feelings about your own childhood experiences. This can open old wounds or cause fresh ones that consume a lot of mental energy.

Try this meditation to help clear your thoughts. Forgiveness is simply releasing your feelings of vengeance and resentment. It does not mean that you excuse people from responsibility for harm or loosen boundaries, only that you stop letting the energy of it take up space in your body.

You may find that multiple sessions are needed, and that's fine. Talk to a professional if you have trauma in this area.

1. Find a comfortable position, close your eyes, and notice your breath as you inhale and exhale.

2. Imagine the person you want to release your feelings around. Acknowledge any tension or physical sensations that come up and breathe into them.

3. When you feel ready, imagine a warm white light illuminating your heart. Picture the light growing with each inhale, soaking into all the places where tension arose a minute ago.

4. Next, picture sending a single beam of light from your heart out to the person you have feelings about. Let their body be suffused with light as well.

5. Now send them a pulse of energy and say to yourself, "I release any anger and resentment I still hold toward you. Those feelings were meant to keep me safe."

6. Let the light and their image fade and go back to your breath. Notice if your body feels any different.

Healing Your Inner Child

The strongest reactions parents usually have are due to their own childhood experiences. Even if you are parenting intentionally, allowing your child to do things that you were punished for at that age can be triggering (see the "Know Your Triggers" practice in chapter 3, page 77).

In addition to identifying those triggers, you can also mindfully bring the past into the present to address your inner child who reacts to those situations. It may sound backward since mindfulness is about right now, but the goal is to address your reactions, which are reflexes created in the past.

1. Find a comfortable seat and close your eyes. Notice your breath as you inhale and exhale.

2. Picture yourself as a child and hold that image in your mind.

3. Imagine a time as a child when you were upset. Ask your child-self what they need to hear.

4. Tell them what they need. Maybe it's, "You are enough. You are loved just as you are. You're safe. You're not responsible for anyone else's feelings." Send that message to your inner child with love.

5. Continue breathing that energy toward your inner child until your time is up or you feel complete.

Beautiful Boundaries

Children force you to examine your priorities and make tough choices about time management and relationships. This is especially true for single parents, those in the role of primary caregiver, and parents in multigenerational homes, as their options may be more limited, and they're under more pressure to keep everyone else happy.

Boundaries aren't about refusing to help others; they just let people know what is and isn't okay. If a boundary is new, people may push back on it, just like toddlers. How do you decide where to draw the line?

1. Get a pen and paper, open a digital document, or open a voice recording program, and find a comfortable place to be.

2. Answer these prompts:

   A. How are you currently spending your time?

   B. What activities are causing resentment, avoidance, frustration, or stress?

   C. Why did you agree to participate?

   D. What boundary do you need to set to protect your time and energy?

3. Some activities could be work-related projects that can't be avoided, but some adjustments could be made. Others might be volunteer positions where you didn't want to disappoint people or felt too guilty to say no. What can you back out of? What shifts would make these activities work for you?

4. Stay aware of how these particular commitments affect you and where firm boundaries may be required.

— Visualize Your Parenting Village —

Modern societies often value independence and self-sufficiency above all else. If it feels like you can't keep up, that's because it's not possible to do everything on your own. Asking for help can be difficult, and you may not even know what support you need. There are a plethora of parenting resources and ways to connect with other families, and when you need in-person support, online friends count, too. Reach out and cultivate these relationships.

1. Find a comfortable position and close your eyes. Focus on your breath going in and out.

2. Imagine you and your child walking together in a small community. You feel safe and supported and you know everyone there. Notice how that feels.

3. As you see yourself walking, notice who is there that you recognize. What role do they play in your life right now?

4. Now notice if there are people you don't know. What kind of support do they offer in your visualization? What kind of people do you still need in your life?

5. On your inhales, breathe in that sense of community care. On your exhales, breathe out connection and love.

Ask for Help

Intellectually, you probably know that you could use help. In practice, it may be a different story. Asking for help can feel vulnerable or like admitting failure, but it's not. Most people are happy to offer help when they can but resist asking for it to avoid feeling needy.

This may sound like a strange mindfulness activity, but have you ever investigated the feelings that arise when you need help? Here's your chance.

1. Find a comfortable seated position and close your eyes. Breathe normally for a few cycles, simply observing your breath.

2. Now think back to a time someone asked you for help. How did you feel? Proud? Happy? Relieved? Acknowledge those feelings. It often feels good to be able to support someone else.

3. Next, think of a time you needed help. What feelings come up? Where do you feel those feelings in your body? Are those the same feelings as when you can offer help, or are they feelings of shame or weakness? Breathe into any tension in your body, acknowledge those feelings, and release them.

4. Return to this meditation when you need support and are struggling to ask.

The Digital Age

Does your child think you have a black rectangle permanently in front of your face because you're always on your phone? Phones contain all the things you like, and they don't need snacks. There's no inherent problem with technology use. It's incredible to have so much information at your fingertips, but it can be easy to tune out from your kids and tune into tech. If you have this under control, you're amazing. If not, you're not alone.

1. Start by just observing how often you reach for your phone. You may want to go into your device settings and check your daily screen time use just to get a baseline. If you have a strong reaction to it, notice that.

2. With that information, consider if you're comfortable with that amount of time or not. Maybe using your phone for work allows you to spend more time with your kids, or maybe it's a distraction. What's true for you?

3. If you're happy with your screen use, try telling your child what you're doing when you use your phone: "I'm emailing a client" or "I'm texting Grandma about dinner."

4. If you would like to cut down, try setting app timers for social media or games, or giving yourself set hours to use your phone.

Managing Unsolicited Advice

When someone offers unsolicited advice that conflicts with your values, it can bring up defensive feelings. You want to justify your reasoning and pull out your prepared slides with citations and graphs to combat their excuse of "That's what my parents did, and I turned out fine." Then any disagreement becomes personal and no one wins. It gets particularly tricky with family members or people you respect.

People-pleasing is another practice rooted in fear that you won't be loved if you don't behave a certain way. If you can avoid reacting out of fear, you can be clear and kind.

1. When someone offers a suggestion or advice that sounds judgmental, don't respond until you've closed your mouth and taken a breath or two through your nose.

2. Once you've taken that pause, instead of trying to explain yourself, simply reply with either of the following:

   • I'll keep that in mind, thank you.

   • What makes you think that?

3. The former validates their contribution without a promise, and the latter asks them to explain their reasoning, which is often flawed. Continue to focus on your breath if you feel tension rising.

Out of Control

Despite their small size and inexperience with life, children are whole human beings deserving of respect. That may not sound revolutionary, but it's shocking how many people don't consider it. Some people seem to think that children must be forced, threatened, or cajoled into obeying adults at all costs.

Toddlers often feel powerless, so they grasp onto control wherever they can. The only areas they have true control over are eating, sleeping, and toileting, so if those areas become a power struggle, no one wins. If you give some parents credit for their child being a "good eater/sleeper," you're also judging parents whose children aren't so easy in those areas.

1. Get a piece of paper and a writing utensil. Draw a circle that's about 6 inches in diameter on the paper.

2. Inside the circle, write "Things I can control," and outside the circle, write "Things I can't control."

3. Write words in the appropriate places for what is and is not actually influenced directly by you (such as "time," "eating," and "breathing").

4. Next, flip the paper over and draw a similar circle with the same labels. Now fill it out as if you were your child. How many things can't they control?

5. Notice how your body feels and observe your breath. Imagine how your toddler feels with so many factors out of their control.

Asking Practice

Asking for help requires an uncomfortable level of vulnerability and may even cause anxiety if you haven't had dependable support before. Luckily, you can practice and build up your asking muscles over time.

In a journal, notebook, or digital document reflect on these prompts:

- What task or responsibility do you dislike the most? Who else could do it or make it easier for you?

- What feelings come up when you think about asking for help or support?

- What's preventing you from asking?

- What feelings come up when you think about other people asking for help?

- What would life look like if you got the help you needed?

If you experience intense feelings, breathe into them, acknowledge them, and accept that they're simply information.

Reminders to Rest

Modern parenthood is challenging no matter how you spin it. The techniques here are intended to give you more individual tools and strategies to manage your feelings, but the pressures are systemic and institutional. You can only visualize away so many stressors like being a single parent, facing financial hardship, health issues, or oppression.

It may be especially challenging to implement mindfulness practices, even for five minutes, when you feel these pressures so keenly. But there will always be more to do, and you deserve to rest—not because you've earned it, but because it's your right. Use these reminders when you forget.

- Rest is a right.

- My productivity does not determine my worth.

- I trust that my body knows when I need to rest.

- My energy is worth protecting and preserving.

- Resting is not lazy; it is necessary for my health.

SECURE ATTACHMENT

Even unintentionally, you may have started your parenthood journey as an attachment parent. The term has become somewhat dogmatic, but the goal is to foster a secure emotional attachment for your child in infancy. It's not about following specific practices so much as responding to your baby's needs so they trust you to meet them and keep them safe.

This might sound overwhelming, but kids aren't meant to only be attached to one person. Other caregivers are called "alloparents," and historically were extended family members of a village.

Some may argue that it's spoiling kids to support them, but the way children learn to be independent is by trusting caregivers to meet their needs, so they feel safe enough to take risks.

9

Enhance Simple
Daily Habits

Some days with kids feel like they can only be survived. You go through the motions of cooking, eating, and cleaning up, but it all becomes a blur. Habits and routines are helpful to keep you moving forward, but they can become subconscious to the point that you're coasting through the day.

If you can shift your perspective from getting through the day to allowing yourself to experience the day for what it is, you can incorporate mindfulness practices each step of the way. Instead of trying to distract your toddler so you can do chores, you can be present for your child while you get things done. Your morning cup of coffee or tea can become a ritual that sets the tone for your day. Even dishes, laundry, and diaper changes can become experiences instead of unpleasant tasks to get through.

When you pay attention to details, are more intentional with your focus, and add sensory components to everyday events, you can stay present to those experiences instead of going through the motions.

Mindful Dishwashing

Doing dishes may not be glamorous, but very little of parenting is. When you approach household tasks as something to power through, you're focused on the future. If you can mentally slow down and experience the chore for what it is, it becomes less of an obstacle to something else and an experience in its own right.

It's easy to let your mind wander during routine chores like dishwashing. The dishes need to get washed anyway, so you may as well get all the benefits of mindfulness while you're at it.

1. Prepare the space for dishwashing, whether you need a dish drainer, more soap, or a clean towel.

2. Inhale and exhale a few times, then run the water. Listen to the sound of the water as it fills the sink. If you get distracted, come back to your breath and the water.

3. Add your soap. What does it smell like? Watch the bubbles form.

4. Start washing one dish at a time. Notice how the water feels on your hands, the weight of each dish and its texture.

5. Wash each dish thoroughly and rinse with cool water.

6. Leave each dish to drain, or dry with a clean towel. Appreciate the clean dishes and space you've created.

Setting the Table

It's not always possible to sit down for family meals, but when it is, you might rush through meals to get to bath and bedtime. When you focus on staying present and connected while eating, even a quick meal can feel restorative.

Setting the table (preferably with your toddler's help) adds a transitional activity before sitting down to eat. It's not about using fancy dishes, and you can do this with paper plates if that's what you have. The goal is just to set a scene for a mindful meal.

1. If appropriate, let your child choose a tablecloth or placemats. Find a seasonal centerpiece, flowers, or candles to add ambience if you like.

2. Carrying dishes is actually a wonderful heavy work activity that helps kids feel grounded, but safety will depend on the child.

3. Choose a seat for each diner and have your child put a placemat (if applicable), plate, utensils, and glass at each place.

4. It's often easier to dish up food in the kitchen, but if there's space, serve food at the table and allow your toddler to serve themself if it's safe.

Strategic Scheduling

Do your days feel purposeful, or simply busy? You may feel pressure to sign your child up for groups and classes, take them to events, and find plenty of enrichment activities. Maybe you feel obligated to attend family functions during naptime or bedtime.

Children need more time to process experiences than adults do, and adults need some space as well. Constantly feeling busy may seem productive, but it can lead to stress and burnout. It may sound like you need to fill your toddler's days with stimulation, but simply going about daily life is educational for them. Check in with yourself when choosing what gets on your calendar.

1. Before agreeing to an activity, check in with yourself. Do you feel any physical reactions such as tension, shallow breathing, or sensations in your stomach?

2. Are you planning something because you feel that you *should,* or because you or your child want to?

3. Close your eyes and imagine going to that activity. What do you see? Does it seem enjoyable or stressful?

4. Base your decision off those factors, not off anyone else's feelings.

Creating Mindful Routines

Routines can be a double-edged sword: They save you executive functioning energy, but they can turn into mindless actions you perform on autopilot. You can also accidentally fall into routines that aren't serving you, and then it's a habit you must break.

Instead, think about what habits you want to create and intentionally plan for them. This could even be making space for a daily meditation practice. While rules can feel restrictive, having some structure allows you to focus more on the actions within it.

1. Think of a habit you want to cultivate. Close your eyes and imagine yourself performing that task. When is it? Where? How do you remember? What comes before and after it?

2. What do you need to start this habit? A reminder from a friend, an alarm, or a sticky note where you'll see it?

3. What is the benefit of this habit? If you stay connected to the purpose of an action, you're more likely to stick with it.

4. Take the first step to creating that new habit, whether it's doing the task or writing it down. Remember, if you miss it, just try again. Like mindfulness, it's about practicing and cultivating awareness.

Play Observation

Children and adults don't always have overlapping interests. Kids are learning and having new experiences all the time while adults have a few decades of understanding wheels and gravity. That can sometimes make playing with young kids tedious—in the same way that young kids hate when their parents try to work or sleep in front of them.

Being bored of toddler toys doesn't mean you don't love your child. But tuning in for a few minutes can let you appreciate your little one more and enjoy this stage instead of wishing for it to pass quickly.

1. When your child is playing, simply watch them. You can practically see toddlers getting smarter as they figure things out. Observe how they navigate new challenges or approach a task.

2. It can be tempting to join them or try to make something easier for them but resist the urge. See what happens if they get stuck or make a mistake. When they succeed, look at their expression without jumping in to praise them.

Your Daily Soundtrack

Music has an incredible impact on your mood. Just think about how important movie soundtracks are for setting the mood. Some people love background music; others can't focus with that much noise. But you can take this information and apply what works for you.

Similar to aromatherapy, changing up the soundtrack for a task can change your approach and make it feel new again. Try one of the ideas below and see how it goes for you.

1. Add music to a task that needs to get done, but you've been avoiding. Try adding thumping bass while you fold laundry, or relaxing music while you're cooking dinner.

2. If you do want some background music, try looking up "serotonin music" to help you focus. It also works as background music for meditating if that appeals to you.

3. Make a cleaning playlist with upbeat music and encourage your toddler to help.

4. Have a dance party with your child to help increase endorphins and release stress.

Increase Your Joy

This exercise is meant to help you acknowledge and allow yourself to feel joy in your life so that you notice it more. Some examples are a refreshingly cool drink on a hot day, sitting on a wonderfully comfortable chair, seeing a friend, or hearing a beautiful song.

1. As you go through your day, pay attention to when you feel joy. When you do, pause for a moment and just sit with that feeling. Let it wash over you, closing your eyes if safe and possible. Write it down if that appeals to you.

2. When you have a few minutes, find a comfortable seat and close your eyes. First notice your breath as you inhale and exhale.

3. Next, recall those moments of joy. Remember how that felt in your body. If other thoughts intrude, simply notice them and let them pass through.

4. Hold that feeling and tune into more moments of joy in your life.

Indoor Picnics

Teaching your child manners and etiquette is part of parenting, but sometimes you can't focus on both table manners and getting a toddler to eat. Mealtimes can be hectic due to multitasking, timing, or low blood sugar.

When most of your energy is devoted to convincing your child to sit in their chair, stay at the table, and eat with utensils, it's easy to forget that mealtimes are about eating together. Many parents find mealtimes stressful. Changing the environment can help everyone be more present thanks to the novelty.

1. Set a blanket or sheet on the floor, both to protect the floor from spills, and to create an eating area.

2. Set your dishes and silverware on the blanket, sit down, and eat there. Observe the room from this perspective and notice if anything feels different.

3. Notice if your child is more willing to sit, or if they wander and come back. Then note your own reactions to their behavior. Enjoy your picnic!

Interrupted Breathing

This technique is inspired by *viloma pranayama* ("against the wave") from yoga and can relieve anxiety and tension. Since it can be done while seated or lying down, it's a lovely way to relax before bed or while your little one is napping or playing on the floor nearby. They may even join you.

Like any breathing exercise, check with your health care provider if you have COPD, lung issues, or other medical conditions where this may be contraindicated. Discontinue if you feel lightheaded, dizzy, or anxious.

1. Find a comfortable seat or lie down. Imagine your lungs divided into thirds: bottom, middle, and top.

2. Start your inhale. Your midsection should lift as you fill up your lungs near the lowest ribs. Pause for two or three seconds.

3. Next, continue to inhale into the middle third of the lungs. Breathe into your chest, side ribs, and back, and your breastbone will start to lift. Pause for a couple of seconds.

4. Now inhale into the top third of the lungs. The air should fill under your breastbone and collarbone. Try to fill your lungs to capacity but avoid inhaling to the point of tension in your body. Pause for a few seconds.

5. Exhale one long, smooth breath. Breathe normally for a few cycles, then repeat steps 2 through 5.

Everyday Aromatherapy

Some smells evoke strong feelings or memories, while others you barely notice anymore. Simply shifting your attention to the aromas you encounter throughout the day can bring you more into the present moment.

Begin with a few stronger smells for practice, then try to tune into one or two subtle scents each day. Of course, some strong smells will be unpleasant, so aim for scents you like. Maybe it's the smell of toast in the morning, your shampoo in the shower, or some flowers you pass on the way into work.

If you can't smell, choose flavors, textures, or sounds to focus on for the day, and adjust as needed.

1. When you come across a smell you like, breathe it in deeply and (if it's safe) close your eyes. Continue to inhale through your nose to fully experience the scent.

2. Notice what thoughts, feelings, or memories come up for you when you focus on that smell. Acknowledge any sensations that come up in your body.

3. Accept without judgment any associations or thoughts that arise with the smell.

4. Bring your attention back to the act of smelling and breathing, then open your eyes.

Tea-Time for the Soul

Many cultures have an afternoon tradition of taking a break, whether it's a nap or stopping for tea. If you tend to feel an energy slump in the afternoon, why not turn it into a mindful moment?

If you don't drink tea, substitute another beverage, and modify as needed. What matters is your intention and presence. Caffeine and sugar can be a physical pick-me-up, but adding a layer of mindfulness can give you a boost of mental and emotional strength as well.

1. Choose a mug or teacup, preferably one that you particularly like, and select your tea. You may have a favorite in mind, or you may want to spend a moment taking stock of your options before you choose.

2. Heat water using your preferred method and pour over the tea. Watch the water change as it hits the tea leaves.

3. If you can, focus on your breathing as the tea steeps. When it's done, add milk, sugar, or honey if desired. Watch how the tea changes color and how it swirls when stirred.

4. Now wrap your hands around your teacup and feel the warmth on your skin. Close your eyes and smell the tea. What scents can you identify? Inhale through your nose and relax as you exhale.

5. Take a small sip and feel the warmth of the tea on your tongue. What flavors can you sense now? Try to pay attention to as many sips as you can.

Let Yourself Play

Psychologist Mihály Csíkszentmihályi coined the term "flow" to describe when someone is so absorbed in a task that they lose track of time and nothing else matters. Children at play are frequently in a state of flow, yet caregivers rarely are because they are too often interrupted by those same children.

You can also get in the flow zone in a group environment. When you take your toddler to the park, it can be a break for you to rest while your little one burns off some energy. You can also take five minutes of that visit to join your child at play, which benefits you both.

1. When you're at the park with your child, for at least a few minutes of the visit, just focus on them. Chase them, climb with them, or play a game with them.

2. Focus on your own body's movements, your child's movements, and their expressions. Stay present in that moment and don't worry about looking silly or what's happening next. Just be with your child and join them in their world for a few minutes.

EVERYDAY EXPERIENCES

A very simple daily mindfulness practice is to narrate what's happening. This helps your child build vocabulary and increase awareness, but it also makes you pay close attention to your child's behavior and what it means. Just as you work to notice, acknowledge, and let go of thoughts and feelings during meditation, your narration should be factual, not judgmental.

- If your toddler spills their snack and starts to cry, you can look at the situation and calmly say, "You're upset that your snack spilled. You wanted to eat it, but now you can't."

- When your toddler is playing and they look to you for feedback, you can tell them what you see instead of judging them: "You stacked those blocks up so high!"

- When their banana breaks and it sounds like the world might end, you can say, "You wanted the banana in one piece, but now it's in two. How can I help?"

10

The Magic of Mornings and Evenings

The hardest parts of the day as a parent are the morning, the evening, and most of the time in between. But those bookends of the day can be particularly challenging for different reasons. Mornings are hard, especially if your child wakes up before you, because you must start reacting before your eyes are even open. Evenings are hard because there's a light at the end of the tunnel of your parenting day, but you're not the one driving. It's also the point when both you and your child are low on executive functioning and patience. Is anyone hungry? Because then it's over.

You can shift the tone of your day when you incorporate mindfulness practices into those specific times. You can set up your day to start on a more positive note and reduce evening stress and anxiety to improve everyone's sleep. Affirmations can be done while still in bed to set the tone for the day. Closing out the day with a ritual, or gratitude practice shared with your child, can ease you to sleep. Putting your toddler to bed can become a meditation instead of a mess.

Morning Affirmations

Starting your day on a positive note can truly set the tone for your morning. An affirmation is a statement of how you want things to be, spoken in the present tense as if it's already true. Instead of saying, "I want to be happy," you would say, "I am happy."

Affirmations aren't magic, but they act like a mini visualization that adds specificity to help you imagine a desired outcome. While you can't wish your way to riches or better toddler sleep, you can affirm the good already in your life and improve your outlook.

1. Try saying your affirmations while still in bed. If your little one co-sleeps or comes to get you in the morning, have them join you. If that doesn't work, post a list or write an affirmation on a sticky note and put it on your mirror, near the coffee pot, or another place you're sure to see it.

2. Take a few breaths to center yourself, then say one or two affirmations out loud. You can use the same one every day, or rotate them, whatever feels right.

Here are some ideas:

- I am loved. I am loving.
- I am safe.
- I have everything I need.
- I am worthy.
- Today is a great day.

Goodnight Gratitude

A focus on gratitude has numerous benefits, including improved sleep, which makes it perfect for the evening. After a long day, returning your thoughts to the positive aspects of your life can shift your mood. It's also a perfect practice to connect with your child before bed and instill a wonderful habit in your toddler to continue. It's incredibly simple, only takes a few minutes, and has a significant impact.

1. When putting your child to bed, ask them to name three things they're grateful for. It can help them if you go first as an example when you start.

2. The other person then names three things that they're grateful for. You can name more but starting with three is a solid goal.

3. Breathe in gratitude. Exhale peace.

Legs Up the Wall

Winding down at night, both physically and mentally, can be a challenge with so much on your plate. You read earlier that one benefit of meditation is lowering your blood pressure and stress levels, so what if you could add a physical element that does the same thing to maximize the effects?

This is a great pose to do before bed since it's simple and only takes a few minutes. You can even do this in bed if you have the space. Try it as written first, but no one will know if you just do the pose while you're also on your phone other days.

1. Sit down next to a wall with one hip close to or touching it. Lean back and rotate your hips so that your legs are up against the wall. If it feels too intense in your knees or hamstrings, scoot away from the wall until you're comfortable.

2. Close your eyes and breathe into your belly so that it moves gently up and down. Notice any tension or other physical sensations. Direct your breath to those places and exhale that tension.

3. If any thoughts or distractions come up, acknowledge them without judgment and let them drift past like clouds in the sky. Stay there for up to 10 minutes, then swing your legs back to the side when you're done.

Daily Intention

Affirmations focus on who you are; intentions focus on what you do. While no one can control what will happen all day, setting an intention can help you focus on how you want to approach challenges. When you must make one of the many small choices you navigate each day, you can think if it's aligned with your intention or not and adjust accordingly.

1. In the morning, consider how you want to respond or move through the world that day, then state your intention like you're reporting on what happened in the past.

2. Throughout the day, think about your intention and if you're making it true.

Here are some examples:

• Today I was very patient.

• I set clear boundaries.

• I made time for mindfulness.

• I smiled a lot today.

• I felt grateful for all the good in my life.

Progressive Muscle Relaxation

You may be carrying tension in your body that you're so used to that you don't even notice it. It can be hard to relax those muscles, or even breathe into that tension if you register it as normal. Progressive muscle relaxation isn't a catchy name, but it's accurate: you tense each muscle group from your toes on up, then relax them.

Since it's performed lying down, in bed before you go to sleep is the ideal time to try it. Focusing on your body can help you quiet an anxious mind, and the relaxing effect can improve your sleep.

1. Lying in a comfortable position, breathe normally and focus on your inhale and exhale for 3 to 5 cycles.

2. On an inhale, tense the muscles in your feet and toes for 5 to 10 seconds. On an exhale, quickly release all the tension in that muscle group.

3. Breathe for 10 to 20 seconds, then on an inhale, tense the muscles in your calves for 5 to 10 seconds. On an exhale, quickly release all that tension. Repeat as you work your way up your body, muscle group by muscle group.

4. Practice this regularly to interrupt the stress cycle and improve your sleep quality.

Candlelight Bath

Water can be very therapeutic and relaxing, which is why bath-time is often part of a child's bedtime routine. It can also be part of yours.

Adding warm water gives your body sensory input to help you be more present, and if possible, change up your bathroom lighting by using candles (whether wax or electric). If your toddler is the one bathing, turning off the lights and adding glow sticks to the tub can be fun for them. It can also smooth the transition from daytime to lights out.

1. In the evening, fill the bathtub with hot water. Add bath salts or Epsom salts if desired for extra relaxation. If a full tub isn't possible or is too intense, try just soaking your feet or hands.

2. Light or turn on wax or electric candles and turn off the lights.

3. Get in the bath and let your eyes adjust. Feel the water on your body as you breathe. As you exhale, feel the tension wash out of your body.

Tomorrow's To-Dos

Each time you must make a choice about what to eat, how to respond to your child, or how to take a detour because of road construction, it uses some of your executive function skills. You have a set amount for the day, and by bedtime you may have run out.

Planning at that time may seem at odds with mindfulness since thinking about the future might not feel like it's increasing your awareness of the present but sitting with your task list when you don't need to start on it can relieve some pressure the next day.

1. Choose a time to focus for 5 minutes before you go to bed and get paper and a pen.

2. Write down everything you think you "need" to get done tomorrow. You may be tempted to do this exercise in your head, but that will still require you to remember all these tasks, so it won't work. Don't worry if the list is overwhelming.

3. Next, go through the list and circle the top three priorities for the day. If you get nothing else done, which three tasks must get finished?

4. Of those three tasks, which is the most urgent? Write that down first, followed by the other two that are circled. If you finish those items, then you can move on to the rest of the list, but not before.

Bedtime Meditation

Bedtime can become a minefield of anxiety as you try to process your day, plan for the future, think of everything you need to do, and try really hard to relax for sleep. Anxiety is when your body overreacts to perceived threats and increases hormone levels that keep you alert. Those perceived threats could be entirely valid, but your body can't tell the difference between the stress of actual danger and the fear of being late to work. Not a great recipe for sleep.

Using meditation and affirmations to rewire those brain circuits can help you relax and rest.

1. Sit or lie down in a comfortable position and close your eyes.

2. Inhale through your nose, and exhale through your mouth at your normal pace. Focus on how your breath feels moving in and out of your body.

3. Notice any places of tension in your body and direct your breath there, exhaling that sensation of tightness.

4. When your body feels relaxed, on an inhale say to yourself, "I am safe."

5. On your exhale, say to yourself, "It's okay to rest."

6. Repeat for 5 to 10 cycles until you feel ready to sleep. If you drift off to sleep during this meditation, even better.

Bedtime Snuggles

Many parents start to feel resentful around bedtime. After arriving home from work or a busy day, it can feel like a race until bedtime. Your child may have big feelings to process, and while the light is at the end of the tunnel, your little one will not go to sleep. What if instead of seeing bedtime as one last hurdle to jump, you used it as your mindfulness practice?

1. Choose a place at bedtime to snuggle your child. Their bed or your bed may be easiest, but the couch, a chair, or the floor work if that's what's available.

2. Get cozy and hold your little one in a comfortable position for both of you.

3. As you snuggle, breathe in the scent of their hair, feel their weight and warmth against you. Notice their breath as well. See if you can tell when they fall asleep based on their breathing alone.

Self-Massage

Massage can improve circulation, stimulate the lymphatic system, and release muscle tension, among other benefits. The cost and time required can be prohibitive, and many people have sensory issues or other reasons they don't want someone else touching them.

Luckily, most people can manage a few minutes of relaxing massage at home. This version is for your feet, but if you don't like the feeling, try massaging your hands and forearms instead. Do this in the evening after a busy day, or before bed to help you relax.

1. Find a comfortable seat where you can cross your legs, such as on a couch or the floor.

2. Take one of your feet into your hands. Notice any aches or tension you feel.

3. If desired, use a dollop of lotion or a few drops of food-grade oil (olive, almond, avocado, etc.) for moisture. Rub it between your hands to warm it up first, then smooth it on your foot to help your fingers slide.

4. Then start the massage at the center of your foot and work out toward your toes. Go back to the center and work toward your heels. Squeeze your heels. Rub the top of your foot and then stretch your toes.

5. Switch feet and repeat the process.

Breathwork before Breakfast

Starting your morning with a breathing exercise can help you feel focused and energized even before a shower or cup of coffee. This practice is based on the "Breath of Joy" exercise that was introduced in the 1970s and actually takes fewer than five minutes. Combining breath and body movements invigorates the body and helps stimulate your circulatory and lymphatic systems.

This three-part breath is considered an intermediate technique, so if you're new to breathwork, you may prefer to try this one after some others. If you feel light-headed or dizzy, take a break.

1. Stand with your feet slightly wider than shoulder width apart and flex your knees. Breathe normally to get centered for a moment, then exhale deeply.

2. You'll quickly inhale 3 times before you exhale, each time filling one-third of your lungs.

3. On the first part of the inhale, breathe into the bottom of your lungs and raise your arms in front of you to shoulder height.

4. On the second part of the inhale, breathe into the middle of your lungs, and swing your arms down, then back up at your sides to shoulder height.

5. On the third part of the inhale, fill the top of your lungs, and bring your arms down and back up over your head.

6. Bring your arms and head down toward the floor as you exhale with a "ha" sound.

7. Repeat this cycle several times. When you end, stay still for a few moments to feel more grounded, and notice any sensations in your body.

Shower Sense

If you're a morning showerer, make it part of your mindfulness practice while you're at it. Even if the shower is quick, being more present can help you feel more relaxed and alert.

There are a lot of senses at play in the shower already: the noise of the water, the lights, the scent and texture of any soap you use, and the temperature and water pressure. It can be overwhelming for some people, though others may tune it all out. Focusing your attention on one thing at a time can reduce either issue.

1. When you get in the shower, stand under the water and close your eyes. As you breathe, notice how your body feels and if you're holding any tension. Feel where the water is hitting your skin and let that tension wash away.

2. As you wash up, inhale the scent of the soap or shampoo. Pay attention to how the suds feel against your skin. When you use hair conditioner, notice how the texture of your hair changes as you massage it in.

3. Take a few deep breaths before getting out.

4. Afterward, pay attention to how the towel feels on your skin.

MORNING PAGES

Artist and author Julia Cameron suggests writing out three pages of stream-of-consciousness thoughts first thing in the morning. If your toddler is your alarm clock, that may not be feasible, but there's no single way morning pages must look.

Part journal, part brain dump, part meditation, morning pages are like a mental decluttering session to clear out the junk and dust before the day gets going. They can be written in a journal, notebook, or digitally. They're not diary entries to be read again, just a warmup for life. Sometimes making yourself write down your thoughts feels safer than speaking them.

a final note

You made it! With so many things likely going on in your life, finding time to read a book is a huge accomplishment. Mindfulness is similar: You don't have to be "good" at mindfulness practices, because any time spent on them is beneficial. If you have a difficult session, that gives you valuable information about what feels challenging right now. Even one mindful breath can change the outcome of your day.

With these tools, I hope you feel more equipped to manage your feelings and your toddler's, with you now being more patient and centered, and more aware of your body and thoughts. Toddlerhood is one of many transitions you'll navigate in your child's life, and your own, and mindfulness can help smooth the way in all of them. It's not meant to fix anything; rather, it's intended to be a tool you can come back to, again and again, breath by breath, as needed.

By starting this early in your child's life, you're building yourself a solid practice and also modeling those techniques for your little one. It's important to let children see adults as whole people who also have feelings that need to be managed. That's how they learn.

So, take a breath in, then breathe it out. And again. And again.

resources

APPS

Guided meditations can be especially helpful for beginners. Try an app like InsightTimer, Calm, or Headspace for plenty of free options.

BOOKS AND VIDEOS

Brené Brown researches shame. Look up her TED Talk or her books, including *The Gifts* and *I Thought It Was Just Me*.

Mona Delahooke, PhD, is a child psychologist who explains children's behavior through "brain science and compassion." Check out her book *Beyond Behaviors* or her website MonaDelahooke.com.

Psychologist Ross Greene wrote *Raising Human Beings* and *The Explosive Child*. His problem-solving approach is a powerful collaboration for older children. Visit his website, LivesInTheBalance.org.

ORGANIZATIONS

Postpartum Support International is devoted to education about postpartum mood and anxiety disorders with resources for parents and specific categories for historically marginalized groups.

- PostPartum.net
- Phone: 1-800-944-4773 (4PPD); #1 En Espanol, or #2 English
- Text in English: 800-944-4773
- Text en Español: 971-203-7773

Alison Laichter, meditation teacher and mother of two, shares about her journey as a mindful parent. Find her social media links at AlisonLaichter.com.

Learn how to take your heart rate: Health.harvard.edu/heart -health/want-to-check-your-heart-rate-heres-how.

Self-compassion expert Dr. Kristin Neff also has a TED Talk: Self-compassion.org.

Yoga and breathwork instructors:
- Rachel Ishiguro: RachelIshiguroYoga.com
- Tejal Patel: TejalYoga.com
- Jesal Parikh: YogaWallaNYC.com
- Melissa Shah: FindYourBreath.net

references

Anicha, Cali L., Scott Ode, Sara K. Moeller, and Michael D. Robinson. "Toward a Cognitive View of Trait Mindfulness: Distinct Cognitive Skills Predict Its Observing and Nonreactivity Facets." *Journal of Personality* 80, no. 2 (February 2011): 255-85. doi:10.1111/j.1467-6494.2011.00722.x.

Barrett, Bruce, Mary S. Hayney, Daniel Muller, David Rakel, Ann Ward, Chidi N. Obasi, Roger Brown, Zhengjun Zhang, Aleksandra Zgierska, and James Gern, et al. "Meditation or Exercise for Preventing Acute Respiratory Infection: A Randomized Controlled Trial." *Annals of Family Medicine* 10, no. 4 (July/August 2012): 337-46. doi:10.1370/afm.1376.

Black, David S., and George M. Slavich. "Mindfulness Meditation and the Immune System: A Systematic Review of Randomized Controlled Trials." *Annals of the New York Academy of Sciences* 1373, no. 1 (June 2016): pages 13-24. doi:10.1111/nyas.12998.

Cameron, Julia. *The Artist's Way: A Spiritual Path to Higher Creativity*. New York: Putnam, 1996.

Csíkszentmihályi, Mihály. *Flow: The Psychology of Optimal Experience*. New York: Harper & Row, 1990.

Davis, Daphne M., and Jeffery A. Hayes. "What Are the Benefits of Mindfulness?" *Monitor on Psychology* 43, no. 7 (July/August 2012): 64. APA.org/monitor/2012/07-08/ce-corner.

Greene, Ross W. *The Explosive Child*. 6th ed. New York: Harper Paperbacks, 2021.

Hạnh, Thích Nhất, and Lilian Cheung. *Savor: Mindful Eating, Mindful Life.* San Francisco: HarperOne, 2010.

Lally, Phillippa, Cornelia H. M. van Jaarsveld, Henry W. W. Potts, and Jane Wardle. "How Are Habits Formed: Modelling Habit Formation in the Real World." *European Journal of Social Psychology* (July 2009): 998-1009. doi:10.1002/ejsp.674.

Nagoski, Emily, and Amelia Nagoski. *Burnout: The Secret to Unlocking the Stress Cycle.* New York: Ballantine Books, 2019.

Neff, Kristin. *Compassion and Wisdom in Psychotherapy.* New York: Guilford Press, 2012.

Taren, Adrienne A., Peter J. Gianaros, Carol M. Greco, Emily K. Lindsay, April Fairgrieve, Kirk Warren Brown, Rhonda K. Rosen, Jennifer L. Ferris, Erica Julson, Anna L. Marsland, et al. "Mindfulness Meditation Training Alters Stress-Related Amygdala Resting State Functional Connectivity: A Randomized Controlled Trial." *Social Cognitive and Effective Neuroscience* 10, no. 12 (December 2015): 1758-68. doi:10.1093/scan/nsv066.

index